3-21-62

THE VOICE OF THE CHURCH

THE VOICE OF THE CHURCH
The Ecumenical Council

By Eugene R. Fairweather and
Edward R. Hardy

Greenwich · Connecticut · 1962

© by The Seabury Press, Incorporated
Library of Congress Catalog Card Number: 62-8482
Design by Nancy Dale
Printed in the United States of America

1181070

✍§ CONTENTS

That voice of the Church for which we look is not of the East without the West or of the West without the East; it is not of England without Rome or of Rome without England; it is not of the first century by itself or the fourth or the eighth or the sixteenth or the twentieth; it is not of any particular place or any particular time; it is, in regard to both time and place, properly universal.

F. L. Cross, *Darwell Stone* (London: Dacre Press, 1943), p. 353.

ᴥ§ INTRODUCTION

One of the great issues of our time is that of Christian Unity. Besieged by secular culture and attacked on all fronts by new and militant ideologies the Church has come to realize how vital is the necessity to erase the scandal of her divisions. And this new awareness has resulted in more than just "talk." In the reformed bodies large denominations have "merged"; examinations of faith, order, and polity have served better to define the nature of the unity that must be achieved; "conversations" in depth are in progress between almost all of the major religious groups. In all this activity the Churches of the Anglican family are deeply involved. And one of the hopeful signs of progress in the search for some basis of unity is the renewed ecumenical interest of the Roman Church, shown by its increased willingness to participate in conferences and conversations. Most significant, however, is the calling of an "ecumenical" council by Pope John XXIII. Perhaps no single recent act of the Roman see has received such wide approbation as this summoning of a general council of its bishops and other authorities.

The general council, or ecumenical council, is not a new thing. But it is new to this generation. What is the purpose of such a council? What is its authority? Will John XXIII's council be truly ecumenical? The pages of this small book will seek to answer these and other questions. The first section of the book is devoted to a discussion of the meaning of the ecumenical council, and it concerns itself with the possible results of the council just summoned. The second section is a brief examination of the historic councils of the Church, why they were called, and what they accomplished.

The value of this book is twofold. The authors have reduced the large corpus of literature on the subject to a level and dimension easily comprehended by the general reader. Secondly, the study strives to be a sort of guidebook for all who wish some orientation before the press begins to publish the proceedings of the forthcoming Roman Council. While the authors are Anglican scholars and inevitably write out of their own tradition and heritage, they have succeeded admirably in producing a sound and dispassionate survey. It is hoped that *The Voice of The Church* will serve as a useful tool of information, but, more than this, that it will enrich the thinking of all who are pondering the problems and the necessities of Christian unity.

The Publishers

Part One

THE MEANING OF
ECUMENICAL COUNCILS

By Eugene R. Fairweather

THE MEANING OF
ECUMENICAL COUNCILS

ᵇᶠ I

No one living today has ever had anything to do with an "ecumenical council," but every bishop, priest, and deacon has been ordained and a good many of the laity have seen an ordination take place. Since the same root idea of church authority underlies both councils and ordinations, it may be a good idea to start with the more familiar and see if it helps us explain the less familiar. In any case, we could not get far into a serious study of the councils without paying some attention to the Christian ministry, simply because a council is basically a gathering of bishops who have come together to perform one of their major tasks in common.

According to our Anglican custom, after the bishop and his presbyters have laid their hands on the head of each candidate for the priesthood, and the bishop has declared in solemn words the meaning of the solemn act, a significant ceremony is added. The bishop hands a Bible to the new priest, still kneeling before him, and says these (or equivalent) words: "Take thou Authority to preach the Word of God, and to minister the holy Sacraments in the Congregation where thou shalt be lawfully appointed thereunto." By this gesture he makes it plain that ordination is a giving of authority in divine things—the word of God's truth and the visible signs of his grace—and that as the Church's chief minister he has this authority to give. As the Church sees the truth and expresses it in her ordination rites, authority to preach the gospel and administer the sacraments of Jesus Christ does not come to individuals simply from reading the divine message in the Bible and feeling a compulsion to publish it abroad. The Bible is basic to Christian preaching and to the understanding of the sacraments, but it is put into the priest's hands by the Church, and he expounds its teaching and performs all the other acts of his ministry as the Church's agent and under her authority. While every Christian unquestionably has a right and a duty to share with others the good news of God's love, according to his ability and opportunities, the right to act as a commissioned spokesman for Christ in his Church belongs solely to those to whom the Church specifically gives it.

Coming as it does through the Church, this authority to speak on Christ's behalf cannot be construed as a roving commission to discourse at random on religious topics, let alone to force one's pet speculations on a captive audience. Ordination binds the ordained to preach under the guidance of the Church's witness to the truth of the gospel. Sacramental authority, or the right and power to administer the signs of grace committed by Christ and his Spirit to his Church, is given for that one purpose, and does not make the priest a magical personality, endowed with occult powers for use at his own whim. In the same way doctrinal authority, or the commission to preach the word spoken by Christ and his

Spirit to his Church, exists for the sake of that one message and is null and void apart from it. The authority to preach assumes the public and official teaching of the Church. In receiving such authority, the ordinand commits himself to the Church as a community with a heritage of accepted doctrine and admits the Church's right to state the substance of what he will say in her name. The authority to preach and the authoritative message belong together.

We have already seen that the authority which the Church entrusts to the ministers of the word and sacraments is given through the act of the bishop. It continues to be exercised under his pastoral oversight. According to the Church's historic constitution, the bishops are her chief witnesses to the gospel and chief ministers of the sacraments; both the right to teach the faith and the power to administer the sacraments are conferred through them; and the authority to exercise discipline for the due setting forth and receiving of God's word and the right celebration of his sacraments rests in their hands. It is their pastoral duty to see that the message of Christ is presented unimpaired, and that the sacraments of the new life in Christ are faithfully administered. By their proper performance of this duty the bishops tie the twofold exercise of authority by other ministers into the common life of the whole Church. This ultimate concentration of the Church's authority in the order of bishops is a fundamental safeguard of the due exercise of all authority according to the will of Christ and the order of his Church.

The faith, worship, and life of the Church rest on the authority which has just been sketched. If the duly ordered authority to preach the gospel and administer the sacraments did not exist, the Church would not be the Church at all, as men have known her in history; and when such authority is not rightly exercised, the Church is more or less drastically hindered in her work of bringing the grace and truth of Jesus Christ to men. Of course, it must always be remembered that authority is given to the Church for the sake of the purpose for which God formed her, and that its exercise must be consistent with her true nature. Authority exists for the building up of the Church as the living temple of God, and in its essence it is an authority of witness and spiritual power, not of force or coercion. But for all that it is a genuine authority, which by its intrinsic weight claims the obedience of the clergy in all their ministrations and of every Christian in his hearing of the word and his receiving of the sacraments.

The Church's authority to teach finds a rare and extraordinary and especially solemn expression in the ecumenical councils. Their authority in the sphere of discipline and canon law is also important, but not as important as their authority in matters of faith. Rules of discipline may and do change, but the fundamental message of the gospel, to which the ecumenical councils bear authoritative witness, is unchanging. In order, then, to understand the real meaning of these councils in the life of the Church, we must focus our attention on their authority in the sphere of Christian doctrine. Their supreme task here is the setting forth of what are known as definitions of "dogma." (This word need not frighten us, because in this context it simply means authoritative teachings or affirmations of faith.) Thus we can best explain the special function of the councils in the Church's life by trying to answer three questions:

What is the place of dogma in the Christian religion? By what right do church councils claim a special authority to define dogma? How does the dogmatic authority of ecumenical councils work?

᷍ᴥ II

The basis of all that the Church is and does is the reconciling and renewing work that God has done through Jesus Christ.

> The Church's one foundation
> Is Jesus Christ her Lord;
> She is his new creation
> By water and the word . . .

The Church's teaching authority, then, can only be an authority to publish and interpret God's loving action and gracious self-disclosure in Christ. The Church's very existence depends on the birth, death, and resurrection of the Son of God, and her teaching must be built on what she has learned of God in and through those mighty acts in which he restored the true life and revealed the living truth to mankind. Thus a real understanding of the Church's teaching and of her right to teach is impossible apart from a sound view of the nature of God's self-revelation in his Son.

We can put our first basic question like this. The Church claims an authority to teach, and she wields this authority by presenting definite statements of doctrine to her ministers as the essential content of their teaching and to her members as the pattern of their faith. But is the Christian revelation really the kind of thing that can be put into a definite statement of doctrine at all? In other words, can there be such a thing as Christian dogma? If there cannot be, then there is no point in trying to explain the authority of ecumenical councils, since what the councils have tried to do cannot be done. But if Christian dogma is possible, then we can reasonably ask how it is formulated.

Can the Christian revelation be embodied in dogma? I am not asking whether statements made up of human words can do full justice to the reality of God. The obvious answer to that question is "No." What I want to know is simply this: Can what God has disclosed of his nature and purpose be put into words at all? Off and on through church history, theologians have devised ideas of revelation which effectively exclude any recognition of a genuine teaching authority in the Church by digging a great chasm between revelation itself and doctrinal statements about it. Some people, for instance, insist that revelation amounts to God's "encounter" with man in the events of the gospel. This "encounter" may be renewed whenever the story is told, but the "being" of the God who encounters man cannot be described in propositions which even inadequately express revealed "truth." The divine-human encounter does not include any communication of such truth, for a perfectly clear reason: the God whom we encounter cannot be disclosed by means of propositions formed by human minds. It follows that the declaration in speech of the "theological" meaning of the gospel events is not part of God's self-revelation, but is at best an attempt to express and explain man's wonderful encounter with God in terms familiar to himself and to others. (It may be conceded that it is natural for man to make the attempt, but that does not make it valid. We can meet God; we cannot talk about him.) It follows further that the Church and her ministers can hardly have any proper teaching role beyond the bare recital of the story of Jesus. Any authority to declare and interpret the meaning of the story is excluded by the simple fact that the story has no revealed meaning that can be objectively stated.

A diluted form of this view of revelation, which has been rather popular among English-speaking theologians, is really not much better. According to this theory, revelation proper takes place in "events," in which God himself—sharply contrasted with "propositions" about God or "images" of God —is revealed. While the propositions we use to interpret the events are not quite as thoroughly downgraded as in the more radical theory, they remain purely and simply tools devised by human minds to explain the events to themselves and to others. In its more conservative version, this view of God's self-disclosure does concede a special importance to those who were chosen to bear direct witness to the gospel events; indeed, it may even call their interpretations "inspired." But the main point is still the familiar one: the event is the means of revelation, to the exclusion of the proposition or statement. God discloses himself in events, and any statement of the meaning of the events is essentially human construction, not part of revelation— even if it is admitted that revelation only becomes effectual when the events are understood by human minds. The Church, then, may be a wise (perhaps even an inspired) interpreter of the events; but her interpretation, which necessarily takes the form of statements or assertions, is different in kind from revelation. The true form of revelation, we are repeatedly told, is event, not statement.

These ideas of revelation are not altogether baseless. On the contrary, they embody a profound truth. God's self-disclosure and man's faith are not just a matter of God's making and man's accepting certain statements. God gives his very life to man in a personal act, and man responds as a whole person, not just as a mind. Moreover, both ideas reflect a proper concern to exclude a crude biblical literalism—an insistence on the absolute authority of the biblical words in their entirety. Honesty compels us to recognize two things about the Bible: (a) the biblical story presents many serious historical problems; (b) it is difficult, to say the least, to find a consistent religious message in the scriptures, construed literally verse by verse. It is to the credit of the theories of "encounter" and "event" that they take these points seriously. At the same time, they depend on other considerations that are far from self-evident, and in the long run they fail to do justice to the Christian conviction that God has really made himself known to his people in history.

It is not obvious, for one thing, that to say that God acts in personal encounter is to say that he has given us no grounds for talking about his being. It is not obvious that God's nature is such that discourse about him must be ruled out in advance. It is not obvious that human speech cannot be just as much a means of God's revelation as events in human history. (What is quite obvious is that a trick is being played in the statement that "what is revealed is not propositions about God, but God himself." The contrast does not really make sense, because God and propositions about him are not on the same level. Propositions are a means of expressing reality, whereas God is the reality that theological propositions try to express.) And it is not obvious that the only way of escape from a naive biblical "fundamentalism" is the denial that biblical or other statements can be part of revelation at all. Until all these questionable ideas are proved, the case for the theories they support remains doubtful.

Furthermore, the doctrines we are examining undermine the accepted meaning of revelation as God's self-disclosure in a form that can be communicated. We may readily admit that God has made himself known, not by uttering detached, abstract statements from the sky, but by giving his Son to live and die in our flesh.

> Tell me the old, old story
> Of unseen things above,
> Of Jesus and his glory,
> Of Jesus and his love.
> Tell me the story simply,
> As to a little child,
> For I am weak and weary,
> And helpless and defiled.

There is the human heart's authentic response to God's self-revelation—the demand to hear the story of what God has done rather than a bare statement about God's transcendent being—and the Church is convinced that she can meet that demand. But the basic assumption is that there is a story of God's action to be told, and it is just this supposition that the "encounter" and "event" doctrines of revelation seem to undermine.

The real question is this: Do the story and its meaning

come together? If the story as we tell it is to be more than a random series of incidents with no connecting thread, some meaning must be woven into it. No doubt isolated "events" can be reported without any interpretation. We might say, for instance, that "someone called Jesus of Nazareth was crucified at Jerusalem by order of Pontius Pilate"; indeed, unless this simple truth can be established we shall have nothing more to say. But just to say things like this is not to tell a living story. The events that concern us happened in the life of a person, and to make a meaningful story out of them we must know who the person is and what he is trying to do. If the Church does not know this much about Jesus, how can she tell the world a coherent and convincing story about him?

Perhaps it will be said that we can tell a significant story without raising mysterious questions about the more-than-human identity of Jesus. It is obvious, at any rate, that the hero of the Christian story is a man; and if we can grasp something of his human motives, there may seem to be no reason to look further. Admittedly, to have found out this much is already to understand a good deal. But what if we discover that Jesus is trying to accomplish something of more-than-human significance? Surely we shall then have to ask who he is to claim such a calling, if we really want to understand what his life story means. Is it the good news of Jesus Christ, the Son of God, or is it simply the tale of Jesus of Nazareth, a man among men and nothing more? The story itself raises this question, and we cannot evade it by limiting ourselves to a report of human events and a study of human motives. It is true that historical inquiry will not give us more than a human answer to the question of Jesus. But the point is that in this case the best human answer we can find raises a more-than-human question. In other words, the best that history can do to make an intelligible human story out of Jesus' life forces a theological issue on us, whether we like it or not.

Our question about the story and its meaning can now be restated: Is the Church's essential message just a piece of human history, or does it embody a theological decision? Does the Church simply report the "events" as moments in a more or less coherent human story, leaving each man to answer the ultimate question for himself? Or does she tell the story in the light of a theological judgment which purports to state the final truth about Jesus Christ? It is at least conceivable that the Church might merely testify to the human events, in the faith that the incarnate Lord would interpret his own life to believers in an ineffable, mystical intuition. But of course it is quite obvious that she has never done any such thing. The Church's message is a gospel, not a biography. St. Paul speaks for every Christian teacher:

> The righteousness based on faith says, Do not say in your heart, "Who will ascend into heaven?" (that is, to bring Christ down) or "Who will descend into the abyss?" (that is, to bring Christ up from the dead). But what does it say? The word is near you, on your lips and in your heart (that is, the word of faith which we preach); because, if you confess with your lips that Jesus is Lord and believe in your heart that God raised him from the dead, you will be saved.
>
> (Romans 10:6-9. RSV)

Beyond question, this kind of preaching assumes that the divine meaning is inherent in the Christian story. In other words, for primitive and historic Christianity the identity of Jesus as the Son of God is as much part of the Christian message as the outward events of his human life.

To say this is to assert that God's self-revelation in Christ, like his saving, renewing work from which it is inseparable, is something really accomplished once for all. The Christian revelation is not something that must be completed by each man for himself, under some personal and secret inspiration. On the contrary, it is a universal gospel of "God in man made manifest." We need not suppose that salvation through Christ and revelation in Christ are final and complete in exactly the same way. In the one case we find the stark simplicity of a deed done, in the other the inevitable complexity of a disclosure of truth to human minds, and we should expect this difference to cut deep. Nonetheless, it is beyond dispute that historic Christianity sees God's revelation as a disclosure made once for all men.

The conclusion seems inescapable. God makes known his character and purpose in Jesus Christ, in order that through him the world may find salvation. A divine mystery is disclosed to men through a mysterious person, for the sake of all men everywhere. We may fairly ask how such a revelation of unseen mystery could ever take place except by the shaping of a conviction, expressible in words, in human minds—a conviction that might be carried through the centuries and across the seas by the agency of human speech. It seems evident that we must recognize in words and propositions, as well as events, part of the fabric of the Christian revelation, if we are to see the gospel for what it is: the disclosure of God at work among men. It follows that the doctrines we have been looking at are seriously defective as an account of what God has actually done through Jesus Christ.

Can the Christian revelation be embodied in dogma? Certain influential theologies would compel us to answer "No," but it turns out that the basic Christian idea of revelation bids us say "No" to them. Perhaps we shall find a better answer to our question, if we move on to what may fairly be called the classical theological view, securely based on the realities of the Christian revelation.

The classical and catholic understanding of revelation is foreshadowed in a famous episode in the life of Jesus, as presented in the Gospel according to St. Matthew.

> When Jesus came into the district of Caesarea Philippi, he asked his disciples, "Who do men say that the Son of man is?" And they said, "Some say John the Baptist, others say Elijah, and others Jeremiah or one of the prophets." He said to them, "But who do you say that I am?" Simon Peter replied, "You are the Christ, the Son of the living God." And Jesus answered him, "Blessed are you, Simon Bar-Jona! For flesh and blood has not revealed this to you, but my Father who is in heaven. And I tell you, you are Peter, and on this rock I will build my church, and the powers of death shall not prevail against it." (*Matthew 16:13-18*. RSV)

This passage has suggested more than one idea to Christian readers, but surely nothing comes out of it more clearly than the place of apostolic confession and witness in the making of that disclosure on which the Church's faith is built. The inward revelation fulfilled and expressed in Peter's confession becomes the immovable foundation of all that is to come after. Now it is just this estimate of the apostolic testimony that most sharply distinguishes the classical view of revelation from its less adequate rivals.

The main lines of that view can be simply sketched. In his Son God both reconciles mankind to himself and reveals himself to mankind. God's action is complete and definitive, and both the Church's sacraments and her teaching are dependent on what God has decisively done and said. In her sacraments the Church represents something done once for all, and in her teaching she transmits something disclosed once for all. In both cases there is identity between God's action and the Church's action, because it is God's deed that is represented in the Church's acts and his word that is declared in her speech. But in both cases there is difference between God's action and the Church's action, because what God does is creative and original and what the Church does is dependent and derivative. Both reconciliation and revelation are gifts to the Church from her head, not the Church's achievement supplementing the work of her head.

So far so good. But just how does God's gift of revelation come to his Church? The only satisfactory answer is that it reaches the Church in the form of the apostolic testimony. God's redemptive work was complete for all men when his Son was born and crucified and raised from death. But his revelation was only complete for all men when the meaning of that birth and death and resurrection had found expression in human speech. In other words, the apostolic witness to the presence and power of God in Christ was an integral part of God's own work of revelation.

That this point was not lost on the early Christian community is made especially plain by a saying ascribed to Jesus in the Fourth Gospel. The crucified Christ, victorious in death, could declare that his work was already done: "It is finished" (*John 19:30*). But what he has to say about the revelation of truth, in his last hours with his disciples before his passion, is something else again:

> I have yet many things to say to you, but you cannot bear them now. When the Spirit of truth comes, he will guide you into all the truth; for he will not speak on his own authority, but whatever he hears he will speak, and he will declare to you the things that are to come. He will glorify me, for he will take what is mine and declare it to you.
>
> (*John 16:12-14*. RSV)

According to this saying, Christ's chosen apostles were to be the Spirit's instruments in revelation, and it is the Church's consistently held conviction, expressed in the reception and continued use of the New Testament scriptures and in many other ways, that the promise has been kept.

If the apostolic witness is really the completion of God's self-disclosure, and not just the first of a long series of human attempts to understand a revelation made in an essentially different way, more than a little light is shed on the Church's work of teaching. On the one hand, we see clearly why the message of the apostles stands for all time as the primary standard of the Church's doctrine. It is the unique witness to the true meaning of those tremendous events through which God brought life and immortality to light, and Christian thought can never set it aside and remain genuinely Christian. But, on the other hand, we begin to realize that such a high estimate of the apostolic preaching is far from reducing the Church's teaching to insignificance.

Indeed, it should not take us long to find out that, when the apostolic message is exalted, Christian dogma and Christian theology are exalted with it.

For one thing, to say that the apostolic witness is an integral part of the Christian revelation is to give fullest recognition to the religious value of human words. If God has actually disclosed himself through the medium of human speech, his self-disclosure can be expressed and interpreted in the human language of dogma without undergoing any radical transformation. In other words, there can be a straight line from God's self-revelation, embodied in the apostolic testimony, to the dogma of the Church. This is not to say that dogma, formulated by ecumenical councils, is necessarily authoritative. That remains to be seen when we face our next main question. Nor is it to say that dogma, any more than the biblical message itself, can possibly give us direct or adequate knowledge of God. St. Paul's principle, "Now we see in a mirror dimly" (*1 Cor. 13:12*), applies as fully to the most subtle theologians and the most august assemblies as it did to the apostle himself and his Corinthian flock. But this inescapable limitation of all our earthly knowledge of God, just because it does apply equally to revelation and to dogma, is quite consistent with their essential continuity in form. Fragmentary and imperfect our knowledge of God certainly is. Yet in receiving his revelation our ears do hear and our minds do grasp something of his truth, and what has been conveyed to us in human words can be expressed by us in our turn.

While my immediate concern is with dogma, I have referred both to dogma and to theology as expressions of revelation. As long as the fresh expression of revealed truth is the work of individual thinkers within the Church, it is theology; when the results of theological reflection are authoritatively formulated by the Church, theology becomes dogma. We shall see later that the distinction is not unimportant for our understanding of the Church's authority in matters of faith. But for the moment it is enough to get a firm grip on the one basic principle: the Christian revelation can be translated and explained, either in theological statements or in dogmatic definitions, without distortion of the essential nature of Christian truth. In other words, the apostolic witness, Christian theology, and Church dogma present divine truth in substantially the same form.

No doubt many will find this a hard saying, but it can be illustrated and vindicated from the history of Christian theology and dogma. Perhaps the best way to spell out the lesson of history will be to meet a common criticism of early Christian dogma head on. Many critics dismiss the great dogmatic statements of early church councils as pieces of "Greek metaphysics," imposed on a gospel to which they are really alien. But is it true that these definitions stem from a surrender to Greek philosophical notions, carelessly confused by the church fathers with the Christian revelation itself? May they not express an essential concern of Christian faith, even though they use concepts borrowed from the thought-language of Greek philosophy? How else, one might ask, could Greek-speaking Christians have gone about safeguarding their faith?

Let us take a hard look at the phrase, "Greek metaphysics," so casually tossed off by the critics of the ancient ecumenical councils. On their lips it has something of the same ring as "German measles" or "the Continental Sunday," and conjures up a vision of an intellectual disease, to which the ancient Greeks were peculiarly susceptible and which any right-thinking Christian will shun like the plague. But just what is wrong with "Greek metaphysics," that Christians must avoid exposure to it at all costs? It can hardly be the mere fact that it is Greek; there would be no real sense in accusing the early fathers of a failure of Christian patriotism in forsaking the sacred language of Canaan for the profanities of Athens. Then perhaps the evil lies in metaphysics as such. But metaphysics is really just the attempt to get at the ultimate explanation of things, by seeing them as "beings" rather than simply as this, that, or the other kind of thing, and then exploring their relation as beings to the ground and source of their being. It is hard to see what is so obviously un-Christian about this enterprise, which even the apostle seems to have approved when he wrote: "Ever since the creation of the world his invisible nature, namely, his eternal power and deity, has been clearly perceived in the things that have been made" (*Romans 1:20*). It would seem that the real evil must be the combination of "Greek" with "metaphysics." But what is so peculiar about Greek metaphysics? Greek metaphysics, like everyone else's, is about being. Of course the Greek philosophers, being Greeks, quite naturally talked about their ideas in the Greek language, but these ideas have survived translation into other languages and have stimulated fresh thinking in Arabic, Latin, German, and other idioms too numerous to list. In the end, the menace of Greek metaphysics can hardly amount to more than this, that the Greek thinkers and their heirs advanced certain questionable ideas, which Christian thinkers must approach critically.

Thus to say that fathers and councils used Greek metaphysics is merely to record an historical fact. If we want to show that they were led astray in any given case by faulty ideas, we are welcome to try, but vague talk about "Greek metaphysics" proves nothing.

The real questions, then, are these. First, was it (and is it) necessary to use language about "being" in order to interpret and safeguard the gospel of Christ? And then (if our answer to this question is "Yes"), did the early Church, in her use of such language in a Greek dress, do what she set out to do, while escaping the errors into which some of her thinkers tried to lead her? Of course, even if we conclude that she did pretty well in her time, we are free to try to do still better; there is nothing sacred about particular philosophical terms as such. But our immediate problem is to decide whether the gospel and philosophy go together at all, and to see whether early Christian dogma sets a good example of how to put them together. The mere fact that Hebrew prophets and Greek philosophers spoke different languages and worked with different sets of ideas has no real bearing on this inquiry, even if it is often dragged in to camouflage the real motives for rejecting the ancient creeds.

The fathers who lived in the age of the great councils were well aware that philosophical speculation is a risky business, not to be lightly undertaken, and they were openly critical of certain characteristic ideas of the Greek philosophers. At the same time, they realized that they would have to think and talk about the being of Christ if they meant to preserve and understand the gospel of Christ, and they saw that thinking and talking about the being of Christ could not be carried on without ideas and words about being. It was clear to them that no responsible believer could evade one basic question: Is the gospel about the life of a mere man, or is it the story of what God has done through man? In other words, is the gospel the tale of a man who was uniquely inspired by God and obedient to him? Or is it the good news of the eternal Son of God, who was with the Father in the beginning, and yet for our salvation was born a man among men? The fathers showed no hesitation in adopting the higher understanding of the gospel as the message of the divine Word who became flesh and who acted in human history through the human soul and body which he had made uniquely his own. No doubt fathers and councils made extensive use of Greek philosophical concepts in working out this understanding of the Christian faith— though I think it can be cogently argued that they worked critically and subtly on these concepts until they became precise instruments for defining the basic Christian message, and that it was the "heretics" rather than the "orthodox" who uncritically swallowed whole philosophical systems. But the basic question is this. The early Church tried seriously and persistently to work out a coherent account of the divine-human reality of Christ, on the assumption that the gospel is indeed the unique story of a unique person— "the only Son, who is in the bosom of the Father" (*John 1:18*). Many modern critics of the historic creeds, following in the footsteps of a few off-beat members of the early Church, have tried to dismiss the whole idea of Christ's unique being, and have set aside the great dogmas of the Trinity and the Incarnation in favor of a pre-Christian understanding of God's being and a view of Jesus as merely the ideal "servant" or supreme human "expression" of God's purpose, in whom God's "word" to mankind is embodied. It is evident that we have to do with two radically different conceptions of the Christian gospel. Which of them, we must ask, is authentic? If we choose the second, we shall undoubtedly find early Christian dogma irrelevant to real Christianity. But if we come to see the claims of the first, then we shall find no way of evading those questions about Christ's divine-human being on which the fathers and early councils lavished so much time and thought.

If we take seriously the apostolic witness, as it comes to us in the New Testament, we shall not be left in real doubt. For the first teachers of Christian faith Christ's work for man's salvation is so complete and decisive that only the highest possible estimate of his person can account for its value. The great New Testament theologians summon up all the resources of their vocabulary to give voice to their perception of the being of Christ.

> He is the image of the invisible God, the first-born of all creation; for in him all things were created, in heaven and on earth, visible and invisible, whether thrones or dominions or principalities or authorities—all things were created through him and for him. He is before all things, and in him all things hold together. (*Colossians 1:15-17.* RSV)

> In many and various ways God spoke of old to our fathers by the prophets; but in these last days he has spoken to us by a Son, whom he appointed the heir of all things, through whom also he created the world. He reflects the glory of God and bears the very stamp of his nature, upholding the universe by his word of power. (*Hebrews 1:1-3.* RSV)

> In the beginning was the Word, and the Word was with God,
> and the Word was God. He was in the beginning with God;
> all things were made through him, and without him was not
> anything made that was made . . . And the Word became
> flesh and dwelt among us, full of grace and truth; we have
> beheld his glory, glory as of the only Son from the Father.
> *(John 1:1-3, 14. RSV)*

In the light of these and many other passages, there is no
point in arguing that the New Testament is not on the side
of a high doctrine of Christ's being. The person known to
history as Jesus of Nazareth is linked with the Father in his
heavenly life and his divine work of creation. Once this
much is said, the problem of Christ's divine being is put
squarely before Christian minds.

The early Church faced this challenge boldly. The question bristled with difficulties. For one thing, the symbols
and concepts employed in the New Testament itself came
into Christian use from many sources, and it took patient
reflection and deep insight to grasp the one truth they were
all meant to express. Moreover, these various terms came
out of organized systems of thought, which differed from
the biblical doctrine of God and the gospel of Christ at
certain crucial points, and Christian thinkers did not always overcome the temptation to import whole systems
along with the terms, and in this way to distort the genuine
Christian message. It was one of the glories of the early
Church that she found her way past all the plausible com-
promises to a clear and uncompromising statement of the
distinctive Christian conviction that in Jesus Christ divine
being and human being are uniquely made one. The
"Nicene Creed," which took shape in the critical period of

doctrinal conflict, gives decisive expression to this conviction.

> I believe . . . in one Lord Jesus Christ, the only-begotten Son
> of God, Begotten of the Father before all worlds; God, of God;
> Light, of Light; Very God, of very God; Begotten, not made;
> Being of one substance with the Father; Through whom all
> things were made: Who for us men and for our salvation
> came down from heaven, And was incarnate by the Holy
> Ghost of the Virgin Mary, And was made man . . .

It is hard to deny that this statement is descended in a direct line from the New Testament witness itself. It borrows a key term ("of one substance") from the tradition of Greek philosophy, for the simple reason that this term says the kind of thing that must be said if developing Christian thought is to remain true to the apostolic faith. There is no subjection of faith to philosophy, because the faith itself provides the essential point of the statement. There is a use of the language of "being," because this is what the content of faith requires. From the New Testament to the councils of Nicaea and Chalcedon, the main line of Christian tradition seeks to express and safeguard, by every available means, that new awareness of the very meaning of the Godhead which comes to those who live by faith in Jesus Christ, the Son of God. Those who reject the substance of the ancient dogmas, under the pretext of a return to the "biblical faith" from the desert of "Greek metaphysics," merely show that the early Church understood the biblical faith better than they do.

This glimpse of the rise of Christian dogma out of the apostolic witness to Christ is enough to show how intimately theology and dogma are related to the Christian revelation itself. Theology and dogma can really translate and explain the truth of the Christian message, without distorting its essential nature. If we see this, we already grasp something of the importance of the ecumenical councils and their statements of dogma. But the same story has even more to tell us. Theology and dogma do not simply preserve the core of Christian truth from one time and place to another. They enlarge our understanding of Christian truth, by spelling out its meaning more fully and in fresh ways.

We saw earlier that there is a difference between the way in which Christ reconciles us to God and the way in which he reveals the reconciling God to us. The saving act is done in the loneliness and darkness of Calvary, while the divine truth embodied in it is brought to light through the witness of the apostles. This significant difference between God's two great gifts in Christ is reflected in our reception of them. The new life which Christ won for us by his victory over sin and death is made over to us in simple and decisive actions. "As many of you as were baptized into Christ have put on Christ" (*Galatians* 3:27). "Because there is one loaf, we who are many are one body, for we all partake of the same loaf" (*1 Corinthians* 10:17). It is true that each Christian's growth into "the measure of the stature of the fullness of Christ" (*Ephesians* 4:13) requires the constant prayer and service of a lifetime, and in the end still falls short of the goal of perfect holiness. Even so, Christ's living presence is wholly and completely given to his people in his sacraments, that by faith and love each of them may prove all Christ's fullness. It is in this real communication of life that the wonder and the peculiar dignity of the sacraments lie. In contrast to such sacramental communion, our knowledge of God's truth in Christ is given to us through human words, fragmentarily and incompletely. The words of the apostolic testimony do indeed transmit the substance of God's truth, and through them our growth into Christ by living faith and faithful obedience is made possible. But they remain human words, expressing human concepts and pictorial images, and as human words they partake in the essential brokenness of human speech. The one and indivisible reality of God does come through them, but its wholeness has to be represented by a diversity of incomplete and partial signs.

It is in relation to this brokenness of a revelation embodied in human words that the task of theology and dogma can best be understood. The Christian mind keeps striving for fuller understanding of what God has disclosed to it through fragmentary images. The imperfect disclosure of perfect truth rouses the believer to a divine discontent, which drives him to try to decipher the images of revelation. In this pursuit of understanding, he will find himself doing two inseparable tasks. On the one hand, he will have to focus his attention on each separate image, in order to discover what the picture or idea means against its historical background. On the other hand, he must try to see how the images, rightly interpreted, come together to express God's unbroken truth. Of course, the believing mind knows all along that it cannot cut right through the images to the unveiled vision of God as he is. But it cannot be satisfied until it has at least made the most of the images, by looking from every possible standpoint at the reflection of God's reality in the mirror of revelation. That means that the quest will go on as long as believers live in this world of time and space, since every new glimpse of man and his world that the passage of time brings about makes us shift our stance to take account of it.

In this unending quest for understanding the theology of individual Christian minds and the dogma of the Christian Church walk hand in hand. Both what particular scholars and thinkers have learned and expounded and what the universal Church has seen and declared should be our guides as we explore the inexhaustible mystery of our faith. At the same time, we should note a significant difference between the respective roles of theology and dogma. Theology has the more positive task of exploring the various paths along which new understanding may be sought, while the most obvious function of dogma is to block off the paths that have led to gross misunderstanding of the Christian message. This is not to say that the work of dogma is simply negative. In guarding against error by sharper definition of truth, dogmatic statements record the Church's growing awareness of the truth. Nevertheless, the purpose of dogma is not so much to canonize the achievements of good theology as to warn against the serious dangers of a bad theology. For the sake of the deepest exploration of Christian truth it is desirable that Christian thinkers should enjoy the fullest liberty compatible with the maintenance of true religion. In certain situations it may well be necessary to write down the Church's understanding of her faith, over against the radical distortions of "heresy," and we have seen that definite statements of doctrine are quite consistent with the nature of the Christian revelation. But the Church's healthy growth in understanding requires the broadest possible scope for unhampered inquiry and reflection; and an unnecessary dogma, which gratuitously cuts off certain lines of thought, would in that respect at least be a bad dogma. Providentially, the Church as a whole has exercised due self-restraint in her dogmatic statements. As the story of the generally accepted ecumenical councils makes plain, definitions of dogma have traditionally been envisaged as an extraordinary means of dealing with doctrinal crises in the Church, rather than as an ordinary means of theological progress.

The ultimate ground for such self-restraint is not too hard to see. Once dogma has been formally defined and accepted as expressing the common mind of the Church, it is final and irrevocable, and theological speculation contrary to it is ruled out in advance. As catholic Christianity sees it, acknowledged dogma is a permanent acquisition of the Church's mind, second only to the apostolic witness itself as a guide to Christian belief. When the Church has authoritatively stated her doctrine, on the basis of revealed truth and under the guidance of the Spirit of truth, that doctrine stands as a definitive interpretation of the gospel. It is true that catholic dogma, like the biblical affirmations themselves, can be translated into new idioms. In fact, "restatement" (as it used to be fashionable to call it) is in itself not only legitimate but necessary and desirable. Theology has to keep in touch with changing modes of thought and speech if it is to do its duty of interpreting the Christian revelation to each succeeding generation, and as the work of theological interpretation goes on the Church may have to put the substance of her dogma into new forms to meet new challenges. But at every step in the process of translation one question must be repeated: Is the same essential truth being presented? "Restatement" must not be made the excuse for a more or less wholesale surrender of the historic dogmas, under the pressure of non-Christian worldviews. On the contrary, theologians who undertake to translate Christian truth for the benefit of a new generation should imitate the Church fathers by dealing critically with contemporary modes of thought, in the light of scripture and of the great definitions of doctrine, to make sure that in the process of restatement nothing will be lost. Only by such loyalty to accepted ecumenical dogma, as well as to the apostolic testimony, can theology give due recognition to the Church's authority to teach.

We have now taken one long step in our study of the teaching function of the ecumenical councils. We have seen that theology and dogma have a solid basis in the Christian revelation itself, and that dogma in particular has an important though limited role in the interpretation of Christian belief. Further, in noting the historic limits of formal and official statements, we have seen how the Church's self-restraint in the making of definitions does not reflect any doubt of the validity of dogma, but on the contrary presupposes its authority as a decisive expression of the Church's mind. We have thus been brought back, through our study of the meaning of dogma, to the basic issue of the Church's teaching authority, and more particularly to the second of our opening questions: By what right do church councils claim a peculiar authority to define dogma?

◄§ III

Once again we turn to the one foundation of all that the Church is and does. The final authority for Christian faith and life is God's self-disclosure in Christ, God's own witness to his own truth. St. Paul puts the point sharply:

> See to it that no one makes a prey of you by philosophy and empty deceit, according to human tradition, according to the elemental spirits of the universe, and not according to Christ. For in him the whole fullness of deity dwells bodily, and you have come to fullness of life in him, who is the head of all rule and authority. (*Colossians* 2:8f. RSV)

To assert this is to say that all genuine authority in the Christian Church must be securely based on the authority of Jesus Christ himself.

To see how the authority of ecumenical councils is really founded on Christ the truth, we should first look back at God's revelation in Christ and remind ourselves how it came about. We have seen how that revelation was given and published in human history by means of human witness. God's act of self-disclosure was not complete until his divine truth had been embodied, inadequately but really, in human speech. That is to say, the apostolic witness, expressed in a variety of human words and images, is an integral part of the Christian revelation.

Once we have firmly grasped this truth, we can go on to see how the apostolic witness enters into the fabric of the Church's life and doctrine. From the first the apostolic witness to Christ is described as "tradition"—as something "delivered" or "handed over" to Christian believers. Thus St. Paul could write to the Corinthians:

> I would remind you, brethren, in what terms I preached to you the gospel, which you received, in which you stand, by which you are saved, if you hold it fast—unless you believed in vain. For I *delivered* to you as of first importance what I also received, that Christ died for our sins in accordance with the scriptures, that he was buried, that he was raised on the third day in accordance with the scriptures, and that he appeared to Cephas, then to the twelve.
>
> *(1 Corinthians 15:1-5. RSV)*

What the apostles have seen in Christ and understood through the Spirit is delivered to the Church to rule her faith and life.

This apostolic witness or tradition obviously has two sides. On the one hand, there is the act of witnessing or handing over; on the other hand, there is what is witnessed to or handed over. Talk about witness or tradition makes no real sense unless we allow for both these aspects. A witnessing that does not witness to something is meaningless, while a tradition that is not constantly being handed over is dead. Clearly, then, any discussion of the Church's authority to teach will have to take account of both the act and the substance of tradition. As we might expect, we shall find that act and substance are closely interwoven in the Church's life, but it will still be necessary to note an important distinction between them. The acts of witness are many, while the substance of the witness is one. The act of witnessing must be continually repeated if the Church is to endure, but the substance of tradition must remain the same if the Church is really to be the Church.

Let us look first at the permanent content of tradition, since this evidently controls the Church's acts of witness or delivery. When the Church witnesses to God's truth, her witness is based on the apostolic tradition as something definitely given at the beginning of her history. As we have seen, this tradition embodies a witness which is part of the Christian revelation itself. Its special importance as the permanent basis of the Church's teaching is reflected in a phrase that is often used to describe it: the "deposit of faith." This phrase would mislead us if we took it to mean that the apostles had provided the Church with a full set of defined dogmas, all neatly filed and indexed for ready reference, but this grotesque notion is really beside the point. To call the apostolic message the "deposit of faith" is simply to acknowledge it as a definite body of truth, put into the language of a particular time and place. It goes without saying that the Church's work of witness involves the translation of the deposit into the language of other times and places. Nevertheless, the Church can and must return again and again to the apostolic fountain-head of her teaching, just because the apostolic witness to Christ, the head of the Church, is given to her in definite, objective form, by which all other witness can be judged.

In its broadest sense, of course, the apostolic tradition includes a great deal besides doctrinal teaching. Take, for example, the basic pattern of the eucharistic celebration —the "shape of the liturgy," as it is often called—or the threefold ordering of the Christian ministry. These are traditions of fundamental practice which came out of the first age of the Church's history and found general acceptance even before the norms of doctrine were fully defined. Our present concern, however, is with the apostolic heritage of faith and with the forms in which it is directly expressed. We do not need to search very long to find that these forms are two: the scripture itself and the "rule of faith" (roughly credal in character) which accompanies scripture as a kind of key. Nor do we need to look much further to learn that the substance of apostolic teaching is actually contained in the scriptures, and that no other reliable source gives us new content. It is true that the creed, by setting out the essential "shape of the faith," gives us an irreplaceable clue to the true sense of scripture, and that its very presence in the Christian tradition, side by side with the New Testament, is a constant reminder that scripture belongs within a larger whole—the Church's total tradition and common life. But it is also true that the primitive credal forms hardly add as much as a word to the text of scripture. There may be no theological reason why the whole content of the apostolic witness should be sufficiently recorded in written form at all, let alone in twenty-seven specimens of the literary output of the primitive Church. (The Old Testament is left out of account here, since it is the presupposition rather the outcome of apostolic teaching.) At the same time, it is evident that a written text provides much greater security than oral tradition against corruption of the original message, and in fact we have no evidence for the preservation of any apostolic teachings that are not contained in the New Testament.

The apostolic tradition as a whole—tradition of faith, tradition of sacraments, tradition of ministry—is an expression of the will of Christ, the head, for the Church which is his body. As such, it must dominate the life and thought of the historical Church in each age. But it does not follow that the scripture, or any other element of the apostolic tradition, is simply "above" the Church, so that the individual believer can appeal to it independently of the Church. Christ and his Church, indwelt by his Spirit, are inseparable, and so are the apostolic tradition and the Church's ongoing activity of witness. We have seen that apostolic witness and church dogma are essentially alike in form. We may allow this likeness to point us to the perpetual presence of the Spirit, declaring the apostolic message to believers through the Church's act of handing it over. The truth once revealed is transmitted through the Church as the living, active instrument of Christ and the Spirit.

As a living, active teacher, the Church does not simply repeat the biblical message by rote. Her acts of witness are not merely a recital in identical words of a lesson handed down from the First Century. On the contrary, they are the living presentation of a truth which the Church has made her own, and which she commits to her accredited spokesmen. Thus the truth of God's self-disclosure passes through human minds, and its interpretation is affected by their activity. It is here that the problem of the Church's teaching authority becomes apparent. The Christian faith is the Church's faith, not just the biblical faith. But how does the Church make the truth of the gospel her own truth? How does she safeguard the apostolic message in her own continuing witness? What special responsibility and authority do her chief pastors, the bishops, have for the shaping of her teaching?

Once more we must look back at the apostles—Christ's intimate disciples and the other leaders of the primitive

Christian community—who played a special role in the events of the gospel or in the declaration of their meaning. As the early Church understood the work of the apostles, they did not merely leave their witness in scripture and rule of faith as a legacy to the Church. Beside the apostolic tradition of doctrine the early fathers would have us set the "apostolic succession" of the episcopate. If the witness of the apostles to God's truth in Christ is embodied in the New Testament, their permanent authority as chief pastors in the Church is continued in the hands of the bishops. In other words, alongside of the apostolic tradition of faith and order which is committed to the Church, there is transmitted an authority to order the Church's life and, as part of this ordering, to shape her doctrine—and this authority belongs to the bishops as "successors of the apostles."

The order of bishops is not a substitute for the scriptures, which stand unrivalled for all time as the embodiment of the apostolic witness, but it is a complement to scripture. We do not simply have a succession of deputy apostles, appointed to pass on their witness by word of mouth, but neither do we have a cryptic book thrust into our hands for us to read without any human interpreter. The episcopate is the commissioned interpreter of the apostolic message in the Church, and it is through the bishops, as chief teachers, priests, and pastors, that authority to speak for the Church is conveyed to others.

As the supreme governing body within the Church, the bishops are authorized to interpret her faith to the community as a whole. The basis of their authority over the rest of the Church is quite clear: while both the New Testament and the bishops belong within the Church and exist to guide her to completeness in Christ, they speak together to the body on behalf of Christ, in the place of his apostles. Of course, the whole body of the Church is called by God to uphold and propagate the faith of Jesus Christ, and the bishops must not act in isolation from the Church's life or from the thought of her scholars and teachers. Nor can one bishop rightly act in isolation from his fellows, as if the apostolic commission were his personal property. But these points do not alter the basic principle that the final authority for teaching the faith belongs, not to the body as a whole, but to the bishops acting together as chief pastors of the Church, commissioned by Christ and consecrated by his Spirit.

As the final doctrinal authority within the Church, the order of bishops must be her chief spokesman for the truth which she has received from Christ. The episcopate can express its mind more or less fully in a number of ways. Forms of worship, for instance, inevitably have some doctrinal content, and in devising or approving particular liturgical forms for their Churches bishops necessarily make a doctrinal judgment. Thus it is generally recognized that the great historic liturgies are important evidence for the Church's traditional belief. Or perhaps a bishop or group of bishops will issue a pastoral or encyclical letter, after due deliberation and consultation. Such letters may well carry great moral weight as considered statements from those who have a unique responsibility for safeguarding the Church's faith. However, there is one instrument for the solemn definition of doctrine which has proved more important than any other in the history of the Church. From very early days synods or councils, both local or regional and general, have played a conspicuous part in the Church's life. Of course, as a rule these deliberative assemblies have not been made up of bishops alone. Lesser church officials, heads of religious communities, eminent theologians who were not bishops, as well as civil authorities and other laymen, have frequently taken some part in their discussions. But their authority in matters of faith does derive from the presence of the bishops and from the promulgation of their conclusions by the bishops in the form of dogmatic definitions.

Given this essential connection between the action of the bishops and the authority of councils, we might have expected to find the authority of a given council assessed quite strictly on the basis of its formally representative character. On this showing, a council in which the whole episcopate was largely represented would have more weight than a merely regional synod. The facts of conciliar history are not so simple, particularly in the period when the primary Christian dogmas took shape. Local councils, representing the episcopate of a limited area, have been tacitly accepted by the Church as expressing her basic convictions, while great gatherings, representing half the Roman Empire and more, have been rejected. Moreover, out of all the councils held before A.D. 800, a small group of six or seven have been generally recognized as "ecumenical"—i.e., of universally binding authority—without regard to the question of technical representation. It seems clear, then, that the authority of a particular council cannot be determined on purely formal grounds. The authority of councils is essentially the authority of the order of bishops, but evidently episcopal authority, however fully represented in a council, does not automatically produce definitive results. To put it simply, the authority of a council cannot be estimated by counting mitred heads.

Nonetheless, the Church as a whole is convinced that certain councils did give definitive expression to the apostolic authority of the bishops. The councils known as "ecumenical" have come to be acknowledged by catholic Christians as possessing an authority second only to that of the scriptures themselves. It can even be said that the very "catholicity" of any Christian community partly depends on its adherence to these councils in their witness to the wholeness of Christian truth. Consequently, it is very important for us to find an answer to our third major question: How does the dogmatic authority of ecumenical councils work? That is to say, how does an ecumenical council express the mind of the episcopate in the Church, and how do we recognize that an ecumenical council has in fact been held?

✌§ IV

When we tackled our first two questions we were able to appeal directly to basic Christian principles. Once we really took the apostolic witness to Christ seriously, we saw how the truth of Christian faith can be expressed in doctrinal statements without losing its original character. Once we learned to take the Church's ongoing witness to Christ seriously, we saw how statements of doctrine may be binding on all Christians. To put our conclusions very briefly: given the Christian revelation as it has actually taken place, Christian dogma is possible; given the Church and her apostolic ministry as they are, Christian dogma can be authoritative. In order to make the first point we may have had to reject certain eccentric or confused notions of revelation, and in order to make the second we may have parted company with what would commonly be described as the "protestant" outlook, but in making both points we were standing with the catholic tradition of Christendom. Unfortunately, the issues raised by our final question are more tangled. When we ask how the authority of ecumenical councils actually takes effect in the Church, we find serious differences among those who accept the authority of both the Bible and the Church. To be more specific, we find what looks like a radical disagreement between those who admit the fully developed claim for the papacy as the final arbiter of Christian truth and those who for various reasons cannot accept that claim. For the first group, the "ecumenicity" or universal authority of a council is ultimately determined by the act of the pope. For the second group, there is no earthly authority above the collective judgment of the episcopate in a genuinely ecumenical assembly, and the distinctive act of the Roman pontiff proves nothing about the definitive authority of a given council. However much the two parties may otherwise have in common, it is evident that a divergence like this cannot easily be overcome.

What we can hope to do is to pin-point the crucial issue, with a view to understanding, if not to facile agreement. From the non-papal standpoint the real stumbling-block in the papal claims is the assertion of papal sovereignty, and more particularly the claim to infallibility of judgment in the sphere of doctrine. As Anglicans, we need not quarrel with the idea of a primacy of honor and precedence, or even of jurisdiction, exercised by the occupant of the Roman see. We do not want to deny that the early fathers repeatedly acknowledged the peculiar dignity of the Roman Church, or that they had good, churchly reasons for doing so. Altogether apart from the political supremacy of Rome, the Roman Church was honored for its Christian pre-eminence as the "apostolic see," hallowed by the teaching and martyrdom of St. Peter and St. Paul and enlightened by their tradition. Nor do we have any real reason to criticize the evident inclination of early fathers and councils to recognize in this august see the natural center of the Church's developing organization, and on that ground to allow it canonical precedence and appellate jurisdiction. What we do question, and must oppose until we are shown good reason to the contrary, is the expansion of the Roman primacy into a monarchy claiming sovereign authority and extending its claim even to matters of faith. The point at issue, then, is neither the Church's doctrinal authority, which as catholic Christians we firmly maintain, nor Rome's historic primacy within the Church, which we freely grant, but the concept of papal sovereignty and infallibility.

Two serious questions, arising out of our earlier discussion of doctrinal authority in the Church, may well be put to the defenders of the papalist position. One of these questions bears on the notion of infallibility itself, and is prompted by the historic Christian conviction that the "apostolic tradition" must always retain its supremacy as rule of Christian faith. The other question has to do with the ascription of infallibility to the popes, and stems from the idea of the "apostolic succession" of the order of bishops as a whole. Of course it is obvious that the two issues are closely interwoven. On the one hand, once infallibility as modern Roman teaching presents it had been assumed, it was pretty well inevitable that the infallible authority should be located in the papacy. Contrariwise, once the principle of the papal monarchy had been accepted, it was readily extended to cover definitive statements on doctrine. Thus the noun and the adjective in the phrase "papal infallibility" fit together very neatly. Nonetheless, the difficulties they present can be distinguished, in so far as the noun impinges more obviously on the principle of apostolic tradition and the adjective on the truth of apostolic succession.

The first question can be put in this form: Is the claim to infallibility in doctrinal judgments compatible with a forthright and thoroughgoing appeal to history? The problem is not just whether the idea of papal infallibility can itself be defended on historical grounds. What we need to know is this: Is the historic faith of the Church really safeguarded by the exercise of an alleged official infallibility? Is there not on the contrary some reason for thinking that the integrity of the apostolic tradition is endangered by novelties, supposedly guaranteed by infallible authority?

Of course, all catholic Christians believe that the Church is "indefectible," in the sense that the gospel can never be betrayed by the legitimate teaching authority of the whole Church, and even that she is "infallible," in the sense that her doctrinal judgments, duly arrived at in council and acknowledged by the whole Church, are final and irrevocable. But the more bureaucratic notion of an infallibility of utterance, residing in a particular officer or group of officers of the Church, is another matter, and non-papal Christians regard it as an illegitimate extension of the idea of authority. Roman catholics, on the other hand, have come more and more definitely to equate final doctrinal authority with the gift of infallible pronouncement through an official organ. Popular Roman controversialists take just this sort of authority for granted, and from this standpoint contrast other Christian bodies with the Roman Communion to the conspicuous advantage of the latter. As they see it, the Church possesses the gift of infallible doctrinal utterance through an official spokesman, whose decisions are final and unchangeable by virtue of his inherent authority. If this idea of infallibility is accepted, there is little point in arguing about the papal claims, since the pope is the only likely candidate for the post of infallible spokesman. But what we must ask is whether the idea itself is acceptable, in the light of the paramount claims of apostolic tradition.

The Vatican Council of 1869-1870 obviously saw in the gift of infallibility an assurance of the preservation and faithful exposition of the deposit of faith, and no responsible Roman theologian will defend the Vatican definition on any other basis. Nonetheless, critics of the notion of official infallibility continue to see in it a real danger that the Church's living teaching may be detached from the historical roots of the Christian religion. No doubt we may pass lightly over Cardinal Manning's insistence that the appeal to history is treason and heresy because it casts doubt on the veracity of the papacy as guardian and interpreter of tradition. After all, Manning was an aggressive propagandist for an extravagant notion of infallibility, which the Vatican Council declined to canonize. We may even decide that Pius IX's reputed claim to be the Church's sole witness to tradition is nothing to get upset about. If he did make the claim, it was in the context of a scolding given to a refractory cardinal rather than in a moment of calm reflection, and in any case the pope's private opinions bind no one. We may note further that the essential idea of papal infallibility does not require the pope to utter inspired oracles in a kind of vacuum, without consultation or historical investigation. But in the end we must still ask whether the principle of official infallibility, however carefully circumscribed it may be in practice, does not inevitably undermine the supremacy of apostolic tradition. In effect we seem to be given into the hands of the present-day Church—no doubt in the sublime conviction that the living voice will neither contradict its historical sources nor, in substance, go beyond them, but with the dogmatic center of gravity shifted from apostolic tradition to the living "apostolic authority." Once the official voice has spoken, the Church's consent must be automatic, and there is no room for historical questioning—or even for significant historical verification. Of course repeated reference may still be made both to scripture and to the earlier witnesses to the catholic understanding of scripture. Apologetics will obviously be more effective if the essential continuity of catholic teaching can be demonstrated historically, while theology and devotion may be greatly enriched by the judicious exploitation of the treasures of the Christian past. But the dogmatic weight given to the historical investigation, as contrasted with the living voice's official reading, of that past must ultimately be nil.

Modern Roman catholicism provides certain notable examples of the detachment of official infallibility from history, fully and fairly considered. An Anglican writer is tempted to linger on the condemnation of Anglican ordinations (1896) as a conspicuous case of a dogmatic judgment on history insufficiently informed by history; but there are more important instances. To the critical observer the modern dogmas of the Immaculate Conception (defined in 1854) and the bodily Assumption (defined in 1950) of the Blessed Virgin Mary do not seem to be on a par with the dogmatic definitions of Nicaea (325) and Chalcedon (451), precisely because their relation to history is quite different. Whereas the ancient creeds explicate and elucidate a witness whose outlines can be traced in the New Testament itself, the modern definitions appear to be real innovations, without adequate basis in the apostolic tradition. It may be possible to argue for them as probable inferences from accepted Christian doctrine, but they cannot seriously be represented as part of the historically verifiable deposit of faith. Nor does the concept of "development," so dear to recent Roman apologists, really help here, since in the case of the marian dogmas there does not seem to be any apostolic seed to develop. As we have seen, the relation of historical event and theological interpretation in the Christian gospel is not easy to grasp, but it is clear that interpretation cannot simply create events—yet this is what at least some arguments from development are asking it to do.

Here, then, is one point at which the "infallibilist" idea of authority is exposed to criticism in the light of a more comprehensive view of Christian truth. It is clear that the genuinely catholic conception of authority firmly asserts the Church's right to interpret the data of the Christian gospel; on this question there is no room for argument among catholic Christians. At the same time, a balanced view of authority must also give full weight to historical testimony. The Church does not need and should not want to preserve her historical claims from critical scrutiny. On the contrary, historical investigation both of the apostolic tradition itself and of its developing interpretation in the Church is indispensable for the sound exercise of doctrinal authority. What the Church can rightly teach now is determined by what she can verifiably claim to have received from her first teachers and taught her children through the ages. Non-papal catholics are not convinced that the doctrine of official infallibility, exemplified in the papal claims, can possibly do justice to the legitimate role of the appeal to history in Christian thought.

Our second serious question to the upholders of papalism has to do with the relation of the infallible "living voice" to the authority of the bishops as successors of the apostles. Is the papal claim to infallibility in doctrinal judgments really compatible with the historic rights and functions of the order of bishops? Does it not on the contrary undermine the supreme teaching authority of the episcopate as a whole? And is not the end result a substitution of a new and less suitable method for the traditional process of doctrinal definition through episcopal councils?

To put it mildly, official statements of the high papalist theory sound rather different from classical assertions of episcopal authority. Two examples will illustrate the contrast. The great statesman of early North African Christianity, Cyprian of Carthage, believed firmly in the primacy of St. Peter himself as the symbol of apostolic and episcopal unity. "No doubt," he wrote soon after A.D. 250, "the other apostles were all that Peter was, endowed with equal dignity and power, but the start comes from him alone, in order to show that the Church of Christ is unique" (*The*

Unity of the Catholic Church, 4). And yet, much as he valued the original primacy as witness to unity, he did not allow this emphasis to obscure the essential equality of the apostles or of their episcopal successors. "The authority of the bishops," he went on, "forms a unity, of which each holds his part in its totality" (*ibid.*, 5). With these statements we may compare the "dogmatic constitution" of 1870:

> Accordingly we teach and declare that the Roman Church, by the Lord's arrangement, possesses the supremacy of ordinary power over all others, and that this power of jurisdiction of the Roman pontiff, which is truly episcopal, is immediate. With respect to it, pastors and faithful of every rite and dignity, both separately as individuals and all together, are bound by the duty of hierarchical subordination and true obedience, not only in matters of faith and morals, but also in those things that pertain to the discipline and government of the Church spread abroad throughout the world, so that, unity of communion as well as of profession of the same faith being maintained with the Roman pontiff, the Church of Christ may be one flock under one supreme shepherd. This is the teaching of catholic truth, from which no one can depart save at the cost of faith and salvation.
>
> (*Vatican Council*, Session 4, 18 July 1870)

It is only fair to add that the Council goes on to claim that the papal authority, thus defined, is a real safeguard and support of the authority of the bishops as successors of the apostles. But this claim is not spelled out and argued in any detail, and it is hardly demonstrated by the Council's further assertion that, since the pope is the supreme pastor and infallible teacher of all Christians, his solemn definitions of doctrine are irreformable in their own right and without regard to the consent of the Church. We have solid grounds for thinking that the basic order of the Church can be either papal or episcopal, but not both together. And we have good reason to suppose that the New Testament and Christian history, if we appeal to them, will provide fuller and clearer evidence for the corporate authority of apostles and bishops than for the sovereignty of Peter and the popes—or for that matter for the direct succession of the popes from Peter.

The conflict between papacy and episcopate has fairly obvious consequences for the authority of councils. If the pope does not merely play a distinctive role in the Church's episcopal organization, but is rather the bishop of bishops and an agent essentially independent of other bishops, then the authority of the bishops in council must be subjected to the doctrinal sovereignty of the papacy. Perhaps it will be argued, in terms of developed Roman canon law, that papal authority really guarantees the authority of a council, rather than supplanting it. It may be pointed out that, according to Roman standards, a council summoned and confirmed by the pope as an "ecumenical council" is indisputably what he says it is, and is not subject to the prolonged questioning and debate which followed so many councils of the early church. But this Roman gift (like Greek gifts of old) should be carefully examined. It can hardly be denied that the advanced papalist theory, which by conceding universal episcopal jurisdiction to the pope makes him in some sense the sole true bishop, drastically reduces the dogmatic significance of councils. We should note that two of the three solemn dogmatic definitions promulgated in the Roman Communion since the Council of Trent (1545-1563) have been papal, not conciliar. The notion that papal utterances, under certain conditions, can claim a final and infallibly binding doctrinal authority, apart from the action of the episcopate and the consent of the whole Church, cannot help but undermine the ancient and catholic principle of conciliar judgment and corporate assent. There is real point to the contrast between the age of the fathers, when urgent issues of faith were resolved by conciliar process (sometimes with less help than hindrance from the popes), and the age of the papacy as we know it, when dogmatic issues are thrust on Christendom by supposedly final papal acts.

It seems clear enough that the papal theory of doctrinal authority is really alien to the basic episcopal constitution of the Church. If we mean to be faithful to that constitution, we must look to the ecumenical councils themselves rather than to the papacy for the decisive expression of the Church's mind. Of course, we must realize that we cannot expect the same kind of conclusive pronouncement from councils as from an infallible papacy. Conciliar definitions are steps in the slow, reflective formation of a common mind rather than final statements bearing an official guarantee of infallibility on their face. But it may well be that the conciliar process does fuller justice to the mysterious nature of the Christian revelation than the rather mechanical exercise of official infallibility could ever do. The whole idea of official infallibility really reflects the legal thinking of the canonists rather than a properly theological outlook. In it the notion of a sovereign authority, able to formulate an authoritative decree or pronounce a final judicial decision, is applied to the more delicate and essentially more weighty and profound enterprise of defining doctrine. If we were truly sensitive to the requirement of this enterprise, we should glory in the infirmities of conciliar action, instead of looking enviously at the illusory security of guaranteed decisions, papal or otherwise.

The deliberative process in which conciliar definitions have their own special role to play can be briefly outlined. The People of God worships and prays and reflects on God's truth, under the leadership of its ordained pastors and teachers. Students of theology press forward on the quest for understanding through research and discussion. Since even theologians, however confident they may sometimes sound, are human and fallible, their discussions may on occasion lead to serious misunderstanding or radical distortion rather than to deeper insight into Christian truth. If the points at issue are urgent enough, the order of bishops will ponder them and speak to them, either in local or in more fully representative councils. The process of study and debate, prayer and reflection, goes on, and in the end the mind of the Church, having duly weighed what a particular body of official spokesmen has said in the exercise of its genuine though limited authority, confesses recognized truth. The result is not automatic certainty, but testimony of varying weight. This does not mean, however, that we are left in long or serious uncertainty where it really matters, since the testimony of ecumenical councils, acknowledged as such, has an inherent weight second only to that of the apostolic tradition itself. The point is not that the Church lacks final authority in controversies of faith, but simply that the exercise of that authority is more intimately interwoven with the normal human process of seeking out and weighing evidence than the advocates of official infallibility can admit.

The nature of conciliar authority is best illustrated, of

course, in the great councils of the early Church which are generally accepted, in East and West alike, as ecumenical (See Part II). For a full account of these councils we must look to more detailed historical narratives, but two or three general notes belong here.

For one thing, the fathers of the ecumenical councils showed a strong sense of the weight of tradition. They tried to judge proposed interpretations of Christian doctrine according to apostolic norms, accessible to all in the historic trust-deeds of the Church, and when it proved necessary to make fuller explanations they scrupulously followed the same standard. Their whole attention was given to the safeguarding of the gospel itself, and they had no interest in elaborating definitions merely to satisfy intellectual curiosity or devotional aspiration. They did not deny that it is legitimate, or indeed desirable, for theology to explore and for devotion to express itself within the broad limits of recognized Christian truth, but their overmastering concern was to secure the foundations of Christian faith. Certainly when they did define dogma it was with the awareness that the Spirit guides the Church to construe and express her tradition faithfully and rightly, and in the conviction that their own statements were used by the Spirit for the declaration of truth. But their prior conviction was that the Spirit who guides the Church had spoken for all time through the apostolic witness to Jesus Christ, and their sense of responsibility to the Spirit himself kept them from defining the faith apart from the clear testimony of apostolic tradition.

There is another aspect of conciliar practice at its best that shows the same temper of submission to the Spirit. The ideal of the great fathers was "moral unanimity" in judgment rather than decision by a mere majority vote. We cannot pretend that a merely political desire to dominate has no place in the story of the ecumenical councils, but we can see how the righteousness of God, working through the genuine concern of Christian teachers for truth, again and again overruled the wrath of man. The Christian conscience cannot readily forget that the faithful declaration of divine truth results from a sincere searching for the mind of the Spirit, and not from human snap judgments. Consequently, a real meeting of minds in the forthright confession of freely acknowledged truth has always been part of the conciliar ideal.

Another important feature of the great ecumenical councils was their rootage in the common life of the whole Church. Their debates and definitions were part of a wider deliberative process, and not isolated events. They met and spoke to safeguard the truth which God's people had received and by which they lived, and when they had spoken it was the thoughtful and prayerful insight of the whole catholic Church that recognized their unique ecumenical authority. Because the same Spirit who consecrates and guides the Church's pastors and teachers indwells and illuminates the whole body, it is in the concurrence of shepherds and flock in one confession of the apostolic faith that the evidence of catholic truth lies. The effective discrimination between true and false councils in the great doctrinal crises of the early Church shows how clear and decisive that concurrence can be.

From all that has been said about the ancient councils which produced the classical statements of basic Christian dogma certain marks of a genuinely ecumenical council can be deduced. A true ecumenical council is obedient to the rule of apostolic tradition; it honestly tries to cut through the tangle of conflicting human opinions and ambitions to a clearer view of God's truth; and its conclusions pass the test of conscientious and reflective scrutiny by the Church at large. From the viewpoint of human expediency it might seem preferable to have some simpler rule of thumb for weighing the authority of councils, but Christian history does not encourage us to think that any such rule can be found.

Perhaps it will be helpful here to contrast a true ecumenical council with a valid sacrament. Careful adherence to the accepted outward forms does assure the validity of a sacrament, and for that reason it is never to be treated lightly, but it cannot guarantee the worthy reception of the sacrament. For example, a man may have the authority of the priesthood duly conferred on him in a rightly performed ordination, and yet his personal lack of faith and love may hinder him from appropriating the spiritual gifts he needs for the worthy exercise of his ministry. Once we grasp the difference between a sacrament and a dogmatic definition, we shall see that the shaping of a dogma is more closely akin to the worthy reception of a sacrament than to its valid administration. A sacrament is an outward action which conveys spiritual life because of God's will and promise, and the personal attitude of the minister who celebrates it contributes nothing to its spiritual reality and efficacy. A dogmatic definition, on the other hand, is the result of inward reflection on divine truth by human persons, and it requires spiritual sensitivity in those who shape and proclaim it. An assembly of the Church's duly appointed chief pastors must certainly be respected, because these are God's chosen teachers of his people. But the most scrupulous attention to outward forms of conciliar procedure does not guarantee that faithful following of the Spirit's guidance on which the ecumenical authority of a council ultimately rests. We must look instead to the spiritual discernment of the whole Church, informed by patient study and enlightened by earnest prayer, to recognize a genuinely ecumenical council whose judgments bind us all.

What I have just been saying comes to this, that ecumenical councils are those councils whose universal authority has been recognized by the Church as a whole, and that no council can make good a claim to ecumenicity apart from such recognition. I must now try to guard against one serious misinterpretation of this view of councils. To say that ecumenical councils must be recognized by the Church is not the same thing as saying that ecumenical councils derive their authority from the body of the Church. The Church recognizes a council as ecumenical; she does not make it ecumenical. In a way, the relation of councils to the Church is like the relation of scripture to the Church. When the Church agreed on the canon of the New Testament, she did not make twenty-seven books authoritative; their authority as the embodiment of the inspired apostolic witness is intrinsic. What she did do was recognize certain books as a unique witness to the gospel of Jesus Christ. Similarly, when the Church accepts a certain number of ecumenical councils, she recognizes them as Spirit-guided assemblies by which the gospel of Christ has been safeguarded and rightly interpreted. Of course, the New Testament was written within the Church and the ecumenical councils take place within the Church. But the one represents the teaching of the apostles and the others are made up of the apostles' successors, and in neither case can the body of the Church add anything to their authority. All the Church can do is recognize and testify to the voice of her head, the good shepherd, speaking through those whom he has appointed to feed his sheep. Ecumenical councils are not representative bodies like modern democratic parliaments, any more than the New Testament is the report of a poll taken in the primitive Christian community. The authority of scripture and councils alike becomes effective in the Church through their recognition and acceptance by the Church, but the authority itself is derived from the divine commission: "As my Father has sent me, even so I send you" (*John 20:21*).

✑ V

Our main job is done, but one question of current interest can scarcely be ignored. If many people are being attracted to the study of church councils, we do not need to look very far for the reason. Pope John XXIII has announced plans for an "ecumenical council," and Christians everywhere want to know what to expect from it—not least because it becomes clearer every day that the Pope is moved by an urgent desire for Christian unity. Since this is a dominant concern today in Christendom as a whole, it is natural for us to wonder what the projected council can contribute to the common cause and whether we can reasonably hope, now or later, to see a real "council of union."

Certainly we have no ground for rejecting a new council on principle. We have seen that councils are a time-honored way of giving clear expression to the faith of the Church, and a council composed of a large part of the catholic episcopate will obviously have to be taken very seriously. Moreover, there is no reason to deny that further ecumenical councils, in the full and proper sense of the term, may take place. Given the present fragmented state of Christendom, we may well wonder how such a council can be held and given general recognition, but we have no sound theological reason for thinking that ecumenical councils are over and done with. In fact, at the very time when the divisions of Western Christendom were still fresh, men were already looking to a general council as the Church's traditional means of dealing with the problems of conflict and schism, and we can only regret that human frailty and sin defeated their hopes. The recovery of conciliar action, as a way of renewing and reinforcing the unit of the Church across the manifold barriers of man's making, is in principle altogether desirable.

As for the forthcoming Roman council in particular, we can reasonably look for certain things from it. We can hope to find charity, concretely expressed in a willingness to recognize the difficulties which the outward appearance of modern Rome presents to other Christians. Perhaps we can even expect that certain dogmas like papal infallibility, so hastily defined by the first Vatican Council, will be further clarified and distinguished from the extreme interpretations which are more or less widely put upon them. At the same time, we must realize that the council will not be what we can acknowledge from the Anglican standpoint in Christendom as a full general council of the catholic Church—let alone an assembly where those large bodies of Christians whose faith and order are less than catholic can make any direct contribution to a wider reconciliation. Furthermore, we cannot recognize the projected council in advance as a true "ecumenical council," because we do not believe that papal summons and approval guarantee ecumenicity, and it hardly seems probable that an exclusively Roman council will gain subsequent acceptance as ecumenical. The council is likely to do a great deal for the internal life of the Roman Communion—for instance, by carrying out further reforms of the liturgy and by promoting the revival of biblical studies—and this inner renewal will be at least an indirect contribution to the work of Christian reunion. Beyond this, the council will probably promote helpful approaches to Christians beyond the papal obedience. But we can hardly expect anything more to come directly out of it.

Granted that the new Vatican Council is almost sure to make a real, if limited, advance towards Christian unity, what should we want to see as a further step? What, for example, would a more hopeful and promising "council of union" look like? Most obviously, it could not be limited in membership by the present rules of Roman canon law. It would certainly have to represent the whole catholic episcopate, Eastern and Western, as fully as possible. It would make room for the episcopate of separated Eastern Churches like the Armenian and the Coptic, whose refusal to accept Chalcedon and other ecumenical councils of the ancient Church seems to be more a matter of historical misunderstanding and emotional rejection than a real departure from orthodoxy. It would probably even find a place for those Western communities which profess the historic Christian faith but have lost or rejected the historic church order. (While councils are primarily councils of bishops, we have seen that others have frequently played some role in them, and it seems desirable that non-episcopal bodies should make their contribution to a council of reconciliation.) Of course, such a council would be subject to the general rule that the ecumenicity of a council cannot be guaranteed in advance, but at least it would provide a setting in which conclusions of great importance might be hoped for, and it is not inconceivable that in the end it might gain general recognition as ecumenical.

Is this picture only a wild dream? Worldly wisdom whispers that it is nothing more. And yet:

> We have heard with our ears, O God,
> Our fathers have told us,
> The work that thou didst in their days,
> in days of old (*Psalm 44:1*).

Surely the remembrance of what God has done for us all through the ecumenical councils of the early Church gives us some ground for hope. In any case, it is not for us to set limits on what God can and will do for his people. Our rightful role is to prepare expectantly for his acts of grace. One thing is certain: such a council of union is humanly inconceivable apart from patient preparation by prayer, study, and dialogue. Moreover, even if a more or less general council of reconciliation were to be gathered together, its effect would be largely determined by its vital links with the actual life, worship, and thought of the separated Churches. As we have noted more than once, councils are part of a process, not foreign bodies suddenly introduced into the life of the Church, and it is idle to expect that a great council of union can meet at all, let alone be effective, apart from constant and prolonged efforts for unity throughout divided Christendom. We cannot honestly call on God to give us what we are not ready to accept.

Let us agree that it is our clear and present duty, in this day when age-old barriers of distrust and misunderstanding seem to be falling, to work and to pray as well as to hope for a real council of union. We shall immediately be faced with a problem which has cast its shadow over the latter part of this study, and which by common consent is one of the greatest and most intractable problems that seekers after Christian unity have to solve. For the largest communion of Christians the papacy is the cornerstone of catholic faith and order, whereas for the rest of Christendom the fully defined papal claims are the ultimate stumbling-block on the road to union with Rome. We can hardly suppose that this critical difficulty will simply dissolve if we shut our eyes to it. No doubt certain relatively easy steps can be taken in the interests of union. For example, the Roman canonical rules governing participation in a council might be modified or enlarged for the special purposes of a council of reconciliation, and there is good reason to think that Pope John XXIII would make full use of his authority to promote any feasible and promising proposal. But the developed papacy would still remain, with its clear and definite claims, and a particular pope's goodwill would not alter the character of the institution. We have seen that popes and councils are, in the nature of things, uneasy yokemates, and it is hard to see how the kind of council that I have envisaged could do its work without an abdication of the papal claim to sovereignty and infallibility. As long as that claim stands, a "council of union" can only be a council of submission.

In criticism of this stark alternative, it may be urged that a better path to unity remains to be explored. We may be told that the distinctively Roman dogmas do not have to be either accepted or rejected at their face value, without further investigation. The truly constructive approach to the problem is to encourage the Roman Church to explain and clarify its modern dogmatic definitions, in the hope that the removal of misunderstandings will reconcile the apparently irreconcilable. At the moment it may seem unlikely that even the most careful explanations will go very far towards meeting the conscientious difficulties of non-papal Christians, but we must consider the possibility that both Roman and anti-Roman controversialists have built artificial barriers by exaggerating their differences. In any case, it will be emphasized, one thing is clear: Rome cannot be expected to withdraw its definitive utterances, for the simple reason that any such withdrawal would be a confession of fallibility— and that is more than we dare ask for.

The trouble with this line of thought is that it touches every problem except the basic one. It goes without saying that we must do everything we can to dissipate imaginary differences. Every time we dispose of a real or apparent difficulty we clear the air for further discussion. It may well be that many or most of the supposed differences between Roman and other Christians can in fact be resolved by careful explanation on both sides, and in any case the attempt to explain is a precious token of goodwill. But to suggest that the claim to infallibility will somehow cease to be a problem, if we can show that the pronouncements for which infallibility is claimed are really not so bad after all, is to fail to take the claim itself seriously enough. If the doctrine of papal infallibility is true—and surely every catholic Christian ought to face the possibility that it is, in view of the hold that it has on such a large part of the Church—then the papal dogmas are above suspicion. But if it is false—and this is the honest conviction of non-papal Christians—then the most persuasive explanation of particular papal utterances will leave the fundamental difference between the Roman Church and other Christian bodies unresolved.

If the gulf is really so wide, can we still hope that it will eventually be bridged? Is it sheer fantasy to think of the withdrawal of the claim to infallibility in favor of a sounder and more catholic conception of authority? Before we decide that the situation is hopeless, we should consider at least two points.

In the first place, we must not assume that Roman catholicism and papalism are simply identical. The Roman Communion lives by the great historic truths and institutions of the catholic Church, partially warped but not destroyed by dubious developments. The outstanding modern popes themselves, with their sincere anxiety for all the Churches, show the same spirit which led the great Gregory to claim the title of "servant of the servants of God." Is it right for us to suppose that the apostolic Roman see, which more than once has risen from torpor and corruption to heights of Christian devotion and responsibility, can never find its way to a reformation of doctrine according to those catholic norms by which it still lives? If we honestly wish our fellow-Christians well, must we not hope that the striking renewal of worship and the impressive revival of biblical study in the modern Roman Communion are a token of still greater things to come?

Secondly, if merely human expectations seem weak, we must remember that we are not dealing with a merely human institution. We cannot seriously suppose that the full reunion of the People of God will ever be achieved by human effort and human ingenuity alone. Our human task, under God, is simply to prepare our hearts and minds for whatever renewal the Spirit of God may bring in God's own time. At the very least, we must do our best to ensure that the doors which have already been opened, and which the projected Vatican Council can be expected to open still wider, will never again be closed. And above all, because we believe it to be God's will, we must pray that "Peter" may turn again from his questionable claims and take up his unquestioned task of strengthening all his brethren.

Part Two

❧ THE VOICE OF THE CHURCH

By Edward R. Hardy

THE VOICE OF THE CHURCH

☙ I

From the earliest times Christians have been convinced that God wills to preserve in his Church "the faith once delivered to the saints." St. Paul, in spite of his own direct call to apostleship, was careful to assert the unity of his message with that of those who were apostles before him—"whether it were I or they, so we preached, and so ye believed." (*I Corinthians 15:11*) Yet our understanding of what God wills us to believe and do continues to grow and develop, and must be adapted to changing environments. So the New Testament also assures us that the Spirit of truth will guide us "into all the truth" (*John 16:12*), and encourages us to listen to "what the Spirit says to the churches" (*Revelation 2:7* etc.) as well as to what has been said in the past. Thus *The Acts of the Apostles* tell us of the Council of Jerusalem, in which apostles and presbyters met to discuss the questions raised by the new situation of the spread of the Church into the Gentile world. Their decision that Jewish ceremonies did not bind Gentile converts was believed to be taken in the power of the Spirit, and was announced with the formula "It seemed good to the Holy Spirit and us." (*Acts 15:28*)

The word translated "It seemed good" is that used in Greek political documents in the sense of "Voted." But as rabbinical assemblies do not propound the question, "What would we like?" but rather "What is God's word in his Law for this situation?", so the question before a Christian council is not properly "What shall we decide?" but "What does God the Spirit wish us to say?"

Though the Council described in *Acts 15* provided a precedent for future councils, it was some time before it was acted on. Unity was preserved by informal contacts between churches and by the travels of the apostles and other leaders of the Church. When problems calling for definite decision arose, outstanding churchmen intervened, less on the basis of formal power than on that of prestige, partly derived from their personal and partly from their official position. In the Latin terms conveniently used for this distinction, there was *auctoritas* rather than *imperium* in the Church. So from Ephesus John "the Elder" guided the churches of Asia Minor, as we see him doing in the Epistles of John. In the document known as his *First Epistle* Clement writes in the name of the venerated church at Rome, located in the imperial capital and consecrated by the martyrdom of the apostles Peter and Paul, to recall the disorderly church of Corinth to its duty, about 96 A.D. Some fifteen years later Ignatius of Antioch, "Bishop of Syria," on his way to martyrdom at Rome addressed letters of warning and advice to the churches of Asia Minor.

Ignatius already had to deal with tendencies to pervert the gospel into a mythical and speculative system, largely connected with some form of dualism, springing from the difficulty felt by the age in believing that the world of matter was really good and the creation of the good God. Those who held such presuppositions could not believe that God is the Creator of all things, that his Son truly became man, or that his blessings are given to us in the visible fellowship of the Church and through the material elements used in its sacraments. Against the complex movement commonly known as Gnosticism the Church appealed to the great institutions by which it has stood ever since, and which may be called the four pillars of churchmanship. The truth made known in Jesus is taught to new believers in a brief summary, based on the baptismal formula of Father, Son, and Spirit, and familiar to us as the Apostles' Creed. Its essence has been recorded by apostles and other "apostolic men" in the gospels and the other books of the New Testament in which, as the Church came to recognize by the middle of the Second Century, God had as in the Hebrew Scriptures spoken his Word to man. The faith is not preserved in some secret succession, but in the common life of the churches under their bishops. In communion with them and by the ministry of their ordination, Baptism, the Eucharist, and the other rites of the Church are duly administered. At the end of the Second Century Irenaeus of Lyons refers to all these points, and appeals to the visible succession preserved from the days of the apostles in famous churches, like that of Rome, which could reckon up their list of bishops to apostolic founders. There was also a succession of personal memories like that which came to Irenaeus through Polycarp of Smyrna from Polycarp's teacher John the Elder, who in turn had seen the Lord. On this foursquare basis the Church has maintained ever since the breadth and depth and fullness of its gospel.

Soon, however, the question arose what was to be done

when a one-sided emphasis—in the technical sense a "heresy," that is a "grasping" of only one part of the truth—came to prevail in this or that locality. Montanism, which claimed new revelations and demanded a rigorous and puritanical way of life, was influential around 200 A.D. Theologians who endeavored to explore the mystery of the Trinity sometimes produced strange speculations, some denying the distinction of Father and Son, others conceiving of the Son and Spirit as inferior beings. Diversities in usage might be equally confusing. In the Second Century the one great day of the Church year was the Easter festival which in those times celebrated the victory of the Cross and the Resurrection together; the churches of Asia Minor observed the date of the Jewish Passover, while Rome and the rest of the Church had shifted the celebration to the Sunday following. Against such divergences in doctrine or practice appeal could be made to the tradition preserved in the great Christian centers—Rome, Antioch, Alexandria, Carthage, and others —and guarded by their bishops. Or the bishops of an area could come together to express a common judgment. The first councils of bishops which happen to be recorded met about 200 in the provinces of Asia Minor to deal with Montanism. So the conciliar technique was brought into use for the regulation of practice as well as for the definition of doctrinal teaching.

A variety of methods were used to guide the Church in the problems of the Third Century. A great theologian like Origen was called on as a "trouble-shooter" and expert, sometimes as adviser to councils of bishops. In the disciplinary problems that arose after the persecution of Decius leaders like Dionysius of Alexandria and Cyprian of Carthage took the lead, partly because they were men of ability and partly because they were bishops of major sees. In Roman Africa dioceses were numerous, with a bishop in every little town; and the custom of meeting under the presidency of the Bishop of Carthage to discuss common problems had existed for some time. The first councils of bishops which happen to be recorded are those which met in various provinces about 190-200 A.D. to deal with Montanism and with the paschal controversy—the former was generally condemned, while in the latter the churches of Asia retained their own custom for a while longer. A council of no less than eighty-seven bishops met in 256 to support Cyprian's denial of the validity of heretical or schismatic baptism. This rigorist position, often found attractive, was opposed in Cyprian's time by Bishop Stephen of Rome, and in later years rejected by the Church at large.

Through its leading thinkers, the bishops of its major sees, and gatherings of its bishops the Church was able to express its convictions on the questions that confronted it. Even these authorities might disagree, however, and in the next decade the Eastern Church was confronted with the problem of how to act when the culprit to be brought to task was himself the occupant of a major see. Paul of Samosata, Bishop of Antioch, a brilliant if eccentric figure, was accused both of worldliness and of heresy—the latter apparently along the lines of thinking of the Word of God as only a temporary emanation which descended upon Jesus and spoke through him. The whole body had to be called on to pass judgment on this badly behaved chief. The first general councils, in the sense of representing a number of provinces, were those which met at Antioch and declared Paul deposed from the episcopate. The civil authority, although still pagan, was involved when Paul refused to surrender the "church house" (which at this period would mean a made-over dwelling used both for worship and as the episcopal residence) until legally dispossessed. His patroness Queen Zenobia of Palmyra supported him for some years, but when the Emperor Aurelian (270-275) reconquered Syria, he referred the case to "the Bishops of Rome and Italy"—that is, to the Bishop of Rome and an Italian council acting as a "fact-finding commission" for the government.

So by this period the factors which were to make up the history of later councils were already present—a general gathering of bishops passed on matters of doctrine and discipline and expected legal enforcement of its decisions. The Fourth Century opened with the great persecution inaugurated by Diocletian in 303. On the eve of it bishops from all parts of Spain met at Elvira (Granada), and adopted a series of canons (*i.e.*, agreed standards) for the life of Christians in their pagan environment. A group of Asiatic councils seem to belong to the years just after the persecution. In the West Constantine was established by 313 as Emperor, and soon passed beyond toleration of the Church to its support. He found it disorganized by the effects of the persecution, and in Africa faced by the Donatist schism, based technically on denial of the validity of baptisms or ordinations performed by those who had yielded to the demands of the persecutors by surrendering the sacred books. Like Aurelian, Constantine referred the legal question to a Roman council. But when neither its authority nor his was deferred to, he assembled bishops from all the western provinces, including Britain, at Arles in 314. The Council of Arles repudiated

the Donatist position (although the schism long continued),
and took the opportunity to pass a number of canons relat-
ing to the new situation of church life.

Ten years later Constantine became ruler of the Roman
East as well. Once more he found the Church which he
wished to support divided and uncertain. In Egypt the Meli-
tian movement divided the Church on lines similar to those
of the Donatists in western Africa. The doctrines of the
Alexandrian presbyter Arius were grounds of dispute not
only between him and his own bishop but in Syria and else-
where. For him the Son of God was a lesser being, super-
human but not divine. This neat solution appealed to some,
while many conservative bishops could find nothing in scripture or in the creed they taught to converts that excluded it,
and yet couldn't quite feel that the Christ of Arius was the
Lord and Saviour in whom they believed. The method of a
general council was resorted to, to meet these and other questions, and in 325 some 300 bishops from the East and a few
from the West took their way to the city of Nicaea, not far
from the imperial residence at Nicomedia and near the
straits across which lay the old town of Byzantium, soon
to become the Emperor's new city of Constantinople.

ᴥᔆ II

A conventional pattern, devised for the convenience of
students of church history, treats each of the seven Ecumenical Councils of the ancient Church on a uniform scheme.
Each is remembered mainly as dealing with some heresy,
which can be summarized in a brief phrase along with the

names of the chief heretic and his chief opponent. The implication is that each council ended the controversy with which it was connected and the Church then moved on to the next question. The actual story is more human and more complex. While some of the councils were devoted to one issue, others were not; each occupied a different position in relation to the relevant controversy or discussion—the more important ones were in fact at the beginning or middle of the story, so that the crucial event is not the decision of the council but its acceptance by the Church; and the religious issues are often associated with the political struggles of the day. The social background is the life of the late Roman or Byzantine Empire, increasingly centered in the city of Constantinople, in which Church and State came to be so intimately united that one can scarcely even speak of a relation between the two. The Christian West was happily able to absorb the theological conclusions of the councils without being involved in their political overtones; while, unfortunately, oriental nationalities which were restive under the political domination of Constantinople came to express their distinctiveness by repudiation of Byzantine orthodoxy.

But these developments were far in the future in 325. The bishops at Nicaea expressed their repudiation of Arianism by a credal statement in which they added to the baptismal formula the phrase "being of one substance (in Greek one word, *homöousios*) with the Father" to express the full deity of the Son whom we know in Jesus. Even though the word was non-biblical, and suspect as having been used by Paul of Samosata, it was recognized as the simplest way of saying what they wanted to say. They also dealt with several other matters. A plan was made for the reconciliation of the

Melitians; a rule, which in principle we still follow, was adopted for fixing the date of Easter, and twenty canons were issued of which several lie behind our current practice, such as that requiring at least three bishops for an episcopal consecration. The bishops then went home, after a state banquet which was for many of them the happiest memory of the occasion. The real importance of Nicaea was not seen, however, until years afterwards, when it gradually became clear that Arian bishops tended to be subordinate to imperial whims, and that Arian doctrine was not only contrary to what the Church really believed, but also incapable of simple exposition. Constantine in his later years shifted towards support of the Arian imperialists, and his son Constantius (Emperor in the East from 337, of the whole Empire from 353-361) increasingly attempted to enforce Arian doctrine as well. The ecclesiastical history of these years is a complex story of the issue of Arian and semi-Arian creeds, and of canonical experiments in which the main question is, to whom an expelled bishop may appeal. The real thread of the story is the duel between Constantius and Athanasius, the redoubtable Bishop of Alexandria, who became the unflinching defender of the faith of Nicaea and of the position of the Church as partner and not servant of even a Christian sovereign. Condemned by councils which he did not recognize as genuine, and five times banished from his see, Athanasius always returned in triumph, a national as well as a religious hero. Greek Arianism really died with Constantius, although the Emperor Valens (365-378) made some effort to revive it, and some of its representatives lingered on in various positions. By an accident of history the official creed of Constantius' day was spread among the Germanic tribes who were then hovering on the borders of the Empire. Arianism thus survived for some centuries longer as the religion of the barbarian conquerors of the Western Empire, who perhaps found it convenient to accept Christianity in the form of a different sect from that of their subjects.

After the death of Valens the acceptance of Nicaea was sealed under the rule of orthodox Emperors in both East and West, Theodosius and Gratian. Much confusion prevailed in the Eastern Church, and to settle a number of its problems a council of the eastern provinces met at Constantinople in 381. Though not summoned as a universal council, the importance of the decisions of this council has led to its being accepted as such, the Second Ecumenical (Constantinople I). It marked the end of the Nicene controversy by condemning the variant forms of Arianism, and the related errors of Macedonianism which denied the deity of the Holy Spirit, and Apollinarianism which thought of the divine Word as replacing the human spirit in Christ, so denying the fullness of his humanity. Its doctrinal statements have, surprisingly, not been preserved, but a document of the following year quotes from its Encyclical Letter the trinitarian phrase "three persons in one substance." A tradition first made explicit at the Council of Chalcedon seventy years later is probably correct in ascribing to it the approval of the baptismal creed of Constantinople which has come to be the commonly used form of the creed of Nicaea—therefore in The Book of Common Prayer properly described as "the Creed commonly called the Nicene." (p. 15) It is in fact an enlargement of the Nicene statement, more suitable for the purpose of general instruction, and enriched by the fuller phrases about the Holy Spirit, of whom Nicaea had said only "and (I believe) in the Holy Ghost." The Council of Constantinople is commonly associated especially with the repudiation of Apollinarianism; but the emphasis, against Macedonianism, on the divine Spirit deserves equal recognition. We may note that our prayer book text of the Nicene or Constantinopolitan Creed differs from the Greek in three points, two of which are minor; the Latin text duplicated "God of God . . . very God of very God" and the English translation in 1549 accidentally omitted "holy" from the marks of the Church (we have it, of course, in the shorter old Roman Symbol, or Apostles' Creed, which is our baptismal confession). The third, unfortunately, became controversial. It is the statement that the Spirit comes eternally "from the Son" as well as from the Father (in Latin one word, *filioque*), which was added in Spain when the last Gothic Arians were reconciled with the Church in 589, in order to remove what seemed like an implication of the inferiority of the Son. Never accepted in the East, the phrase has come to be a point of distinction between Eastern and Western Churches, the resolution of which must await the establishment of reunion between them.

Much ancient Christian thought revolves around the conflict between the historical School of Antioch, with its emphasis on the full humanity of Christ which is united to his divinity but not confused with it, and the more mystical emphasis of Alexandria on the unity of God and man in the one person of the Saviour. Politics as much as theology lay behind the attack which Cyril of Alexandria launched in 430 on the Antiochene Nestorius, who had become Bishop of

Constantinople in 428. Only a general council could resolve the dispute of the Patriarchs, and one was summoned to meet at Ephesus in 431. Actually two assemblies met at Ephesus, one under Cyril and the other under John of Antioch; but Cyril's assembly received general recognition from the Emperor (Theodosius II) and the Church at large, with its approval of his doctrine and condemnation of Nestorius. However the church of Antioch did not renew its communion with Alexandria until Cyril admitted (in the *Formula of Union*, 433) that it is also legitimate to stress that in the one person of Christ there is a union of two natures, divine and human. This acknowledgment of the true humanity of Christ balances the phrase commonly associated with Cyril's doctrine of unity, that since Mary is "mother of thy son Jesus Christ our Lord and God" (as Cranmer put it in the Prayer Book of 1549), she may properly be called "Birthgiver of God," *theotokos* in Greek. In Latin and English this is commonly rendered "Mother of God," but that is properly a poetic rather than strictly accurate phrase, emphasizing that Mary's Son is true God and true Man.

Cyril's successor Dioscorus patronized a further extension of his theology in supporting the Abbot Eutyches, an Alexandrian at Constantinople who refused to speak of "two natures" in Christ after the union, or to describe him as consubstantial with us in humanity, as he is with the Father in deity. Eutyches was condemned at a local council in Constantinople in 448; he appealed to the judgment of the major sees, and a general council was summoned to hear his case. The result was the disorderly "Second Council of Ephesus" in 449, which has gone down in history as the *Latrocinium*, the Robber Council. Victorious over his rivals of Constantinople and Antioch, Dioscorus ignored the protest of the Roman delegate who cried out "contradicitur," which stands out strangely in the Greek minutes of the meeting, and left hastily. But soon all parties turned against him. Leo of Rome had already expounded the doctrine of two natures in Christ in his *Tome* on the Incarnation. In 450 the weak Theodosius II was succeeded by his strong-minded sister Pulcheria and her husband Marcian; and in 451 the best-attended of the ancient councils (over 500 bishops, or, counting proxies, some 650) met at Chalcedon, across the water from Constantinople. Dioscorus was declared deposed for uncanonical conduct, and the theological letters of both Cyril and Leo were approved. Although the Roman delegates felt that nothing more was needed when their bishop had spoken, still a careful statement of the Church's faith was drawn up, commonly known as the Chalcedonian Decree. In this the creeds of Nicaea and Constantinople are accepted, after which comes a precise statement of the Church's teaching about Christ—"the same perfect in Godhead, the same perfect in manhood . . . acknowledged in two natures without confusion, without change, without division, without separation . . . not divided or separated into two Persons, but one and the same only-begotten God, Word, Lord Jesus Christ." The Council also passed twenty-seven canons, largely regulating the disciplinary problems of the Eastern Church, establishing a chain of appeal in ecclesiastical courts and regulating the relation of monks and parish clergy to their bishops. A twenty-eighth recognized the position of the church at Constantinople, the imperial city, giving it patriarchal jurisdiction over the neighboring provinces, and declaring that the church of New Rome should rank like that of

Old Rome, although after it. The Roman delegates, and Pope Leo when he heard of it, protested against this, but it did in practice come into effect.

Chalcedon was followed by further controversy, similar in some ways to that which followed Nicaea. Most of the Egyptian and a large part of the Syrian Church refused to accept its decrees. Nevertheless these Monophysites (believers in one nature, *physis*) repudiated the extreme position of Eutyches and maintained that their doctrine of one nature in Christ was compatible with the recognition that he is truly human as well as divine. One cannot but feel that the dislike of the non-Greek provinces to being controlled from Constantinople is behind much of the controversy. In 482 the Emperor Zeno attempted a compromise in the *Henotikon* or project of union which asserted the common doctrines and condemned any who might have taught otherwise at Chalcedon or any other synod. But the only result of this clever move was a schism between Rome and Constantinople which lasted for 35 years, 484-519. When a new dynasty began in 518 under Justin I (and his nephew Justinian) Constantinople turned back to Chalcedon, which has since remained the position of Greek as well as Latin orthodoxy. The monophysite parties at Alexandria and Antioch gradually drifted into the separation which still continues in the Coptic and Syrian Jacobite Churches. To the monophysites we owe one familiar feature of our liturgical practice. When in control at Antioch they introduced the custom of reciting the creed in the eucharistic liturgy, as a declaration of loyalty to the Nicene faith which they considered Chalcedon to have altered. The Chalcedonian, or orthodox, party would not repudiate the custom when they returned to power, and so it gradually spread through the Church. The ancient creeds therefore now have three uses —as a baptismal confession, as a formal statement of the Church's corporate convictions, and as an affirmation of our Christian loyalty at the heart of our worship.

With the Chalcedonian decree the classic formulation of ancient christology was completed. In a sense it is a negative rather than a positive pronouncement, declaring primarily that the person of Christ is not divided nor are his divine and human natures confused. It confronts us with paradox rather than offering explanations, and is a point of departure for future theology. In the words of the late Archbishop Temple, it does just what a dogmatic statement ought to do; it states the facts.

✠ III

The Fifth and Sixth Ecumenical Councils are commonly presented as echoes or amplifications of the Third and Fourth, and this is not wholly untrue. Nevertheless, they are not without historical interest and theological significance. Their common political background is the natural desire of Byzantine Emperors to find some means of reconciling the Monophysites of their eastern provinces with the Chalcedonians of the areas that looked to Constantinople and Rome. Much of Justinian's reign, 527-565, was devoted to this effort, and he also developed considerable theological interests of his own. The pressure of Chalcedonian Patriarchs established at Antioch and Alexandria still left nearly all the Egyptians and many Syrians unreconciled to the Emperor's Church. But even so there was a certain exchange of intellectual influences between the thinkers of the two parties, such men as the Monophysite Severus of Antioch, who still defended the full humanity of Christ, and the Chalcedonian Leontius of Byzantium, who explored various amplifications of the unity of his Person. The hope gradually grew that some good might be done by repudiating three items which were especially obnoxious to Monophysites—Theodore of Mopsuestia, the teacher of Nestorius, and certain writings of Theodoret of Cyrrhus and Ibas of Edessa, opponents of Cyril who had however been received by the Council of Chalcedon. The "Three Chapters" as this group of one person and two documents came to be called, were condemned by an imperial edict for which the sanction of a council was then desired. This was secured from the Fifth Ecumenical Council (Constantinople II) in 553. The Bishop of Rome, Vigilius, was at the time an unhappy exile in the imperial capital. After twice approving and twice condemning the imperial proposal he finally assented to it.

At first sight the Fifth Council is an unedifying episode, exhibiting imperial domination of the Church from the Pope down, and the use of a theological technicality in the service of a political scheme. Yet on further investigation this is by no means the case. If Justinian desired a compromise, he did not secure it. The Council ratified and enforced the Chalcedonian position, enriching and developing it by incorporating into the Orthodox tradition some of the ideas and phrases which the Monophysites had worked out, such as the concept of divine suffering involved in the fullness of the Incarnation—"one of the Trinity suffered in the flesh." Probably a reconciliation of persons was at this time not possible, but a certain interchange of ideas was at least effected. With a few exceptions, it was an age of recondite rather than profound theology; but it did make its contribution to the movement of Christian thought. Nor did even poor Vigilius weaken his own cause as much as seemed at some points. At one stage the Council was planned as a meeting of the five Patriarchates, in which Rome might have been outvoted, if necessary, four to one. But by his very absence from the Council Vigilius preserved at least the form of giving a separate approval to its proceedings. An incidental act of the Council was the condemnation of some of the wilder speculations of Origen, the great yet individualistic Christian philosopher who has fascinated many readers in later centuries.

Scarcely had the Fifth Council been accepted by the Western Church generally when a new (and last) imperial attempt at compromise was advanced. After losing his oriental provinces to the Persians, Heraclius recovered them in the brilliant campaigns which culminated in the "Exaltation of the Holy Cross," the return of the sacred relic to Jerusalem in 629. But someone suggested to the Emperor that the separated Christians, who had shown little loyalty during the recent invasions, might be recovered by a new doctrinal experiment—forget about natures and reflect rather that in Christ the human and divine wills are united in one. For Monophysites this was obvious, and it was hoped that Chalcedonians and even Nestorians would have little objection to the proposition. Once more the well-intentioned effort fell flat. The imperial doctrine merely alienated all parties in Syria and Egypt and was one more factor in facilitating the loss of those provinces to the Moslem invaders after 639. But with certain modifications the doctrine of one will continued to be propounded at Constantinople for fifty years. Finally Emperor and Pope agreed in repudiating it. After preliminary discussions the Sixth Council (Constantinople III) in 681 declared that the fullness of the humanity of Christ demands the recognition in him of a genuine human will. Once more a rather technical controversy, politically motivated, left a valuable residue in Christian thought behind it. The deity of Christ is an addition to his humanity, not a subtraction from it, and so in him we must see everything which is genuinely human. An interesting detail is that this is the only ancient Ecumenical Council in which the Church of England had a certain part. Theodore of Tarsus, the Greek who was then serving as Archbishop of Canterbury, was invited to be one of the papal delegates, although unable to attend, and Wilfred of York, at the time in Rome in connection with his appeal against Theodore's division of his diocese, took part in one of the preliminary councils held there in 679. Meanwhile in far-off Lebanon Monotheletism retained at least a nominal existence among the isolated Christians gathered around the monastery of St. John Maro, until in the Twelfth Century they found themselves in one of the Latin principalities set up by the Crusaders and, as the Maronite Church, accepted and still retain the doctrines and authority of Rome.

The Fifth and Sixth Councils had passed no canons. Therefore as a kind of supplement to them a council was held at Constantinople in 692 which codified in large part the canons current in the Eastern Church. This gathering is sometimes called the Fifth-Sixth (Quinisext) Council or, from the vault (*trullus*) of the hall in the imperial palace where it met, the Council *in trullo*. It was a purely Eastern assembly, as shown from its vigorous affirmation of such distinctively Eastern customs as the permission of the lower clergy to remain in the married state, even though an effort was made to secure Roman approval for its decisions. It deserves mention, however, in this brief survey of general councils on the same footing as such western assemblies as the Council of Arles or (perhaps) the western councils of the Middle Ages.

Early in the Eighth Century the Arab Caliphate had reached its greatest power, as shown by the almost simultaneous launching, soon after 710, of attacks on Spain, India, and Constantinople. With the repulse of the last by Leo the Isaurian in 717-720 began three centuries of glory and expansion for the Byzantine state. In the following years the Isaurian Emperors carried through a general reorganization of Byzantine administration and law. In church affairs this took the form of an attack on the icons, painted or sculptured images of Christ and the saints, which had come to occupy a prominent place in popular piety as well as in art. The army, used to the rougher life of the frontiers, and partly sharing the aversion to representative art of the Arabs with whom it fought, supported the imperial policy. Cultured civil servants as well as monks and theologians stood on the other side. Nor was the question one merely of discipline. The iconoclasts ("image-breakers") argued that an image of Christ either divides him by representing the humanity alone, or else professes to represent the deity, which is impossible. Similarly we could make pictures of the saints, but not images of their saintliness. Their opponents claimed that this was one more denial of the Incarnation and the redemption of matter. If God has really become man, then that fact may be put before our eyes. Superstition must certainly be repressed, but the presentation of divine truth to human devotion in images and symbols is not illegitimate. In 754 a council dominated by the Emperor Constantine V supported the iconoclasts. Thirty years later the position had changed, and the Seventh Ecumenical Council met at Nicaea in 787 to register their defeat. Its key statement was a careful definition of the distinction between the worship which belongs to God alone and the "greeting and reverent veneration" (*aspasmos kai timetike proskynesis*) which may be given to images of Christ and the saints, as to the sign of the cross and the book of the Holy Gospels.

The Second Council of Nicaea, like the first, did not mark the end of the relevant controversy. There was a milder revival of iconoclasm at Constantinople from 815-842. Finally the icons were restored on the Second Sunday in Lent of 843, a day still observed in the Eastern Orthodox Church as the Feast of Orthodoxy, in honor of the faith laid down by the Seven Councils. There has been in the practice of the Eastern Church an unspoken compromise, so that iconoclasts, like Monophysites before them, have made a certain contribution to the Orthodox tradition. Statues are not used (except for an occasional crucifix in low relief), and the proper Byzantine icon is, as it were, a window into eternity rather than a renewal of time. Eastern visitors have often been startled by the statues and naturalistic paintings they may find in a western church. Similarly westerners are often at first surprised to find that in the Christian East the sense of divine presence in the church building is not so much associated with a conspicuous altar or with the Blessed Sacrament in its tabernacle as with the surrounding figures of Christ and his mother and the rest of the host of heaven.

The decision of 787 was easily understood at Rome, but north of the Alps the distinctions of the Greek language were lost in Latin translation, and it seemed as if the Council had approved of idolatry. Charlemagne, whose Frankish Empire dominated Western Europe, assembled in 795 a Council at Frankfort which formally repudiated what they thought to be the decrees of the Nicene Synod. In due time the matter became clear, but there lingered in western writers a certain doubt as to whether the Seventh Council really belonged in the same class as the first six. This was picked up at the Reformation by those of the Reformers (by no means all of them) who took an iconoclastic attitude towards sacred art and excluded symbolism from their churches. For this and other reasons theologians of the Church of England have varied in their attitude towards the Seventh Council, which has led to a recent suggestion that she should now formally accept it. This seems to be unnecessary, since we certainly act on its principles, properly understood. It would seem better simply to understand that the theology of the Seven Councils is part of the tradition which we have inherited from the days of the undivided Church.

For with the Second Council of Nicaea the list of Synods recognized as Ecumenical by the Eastern Orthodox Church is complete, at least until an undisputed Eighth Synod assembles. Historical accident has thus given to the list of councils the further associations of a sacred number. When there were four synods they were suggestive of the faith of the Four Gospels. Now that there have for so long been seven, the number seems to fall into the same category with the seven gifts of the Spirit, the seven lamps before the throne (*Revelation* 4:5), the seven sacraments, and other such sacred groups of seven. However this has not prevented, now and again, another significant gathering being described as the "Eighth Synod," more or less rhetorically. In the Ninth Century there was a brief schism between Rome and Constantinople when the deposed (or compulsorily retired) Patriarch Ignatius appealed for papal support, and his successor Photius in his defence assembled the various grounds of Greek complaint against the Western Church. Each party had excommunicated the other when in 867 a palace revolution at Constantinople led to Ignatius' restoration. In 869 a Council at Constantinople condemned Photius and his supporters. Ten years later Photius, who after the death of Ignatius came back as legitimate Patriarch, held a much more largely attended council which reversed the decisions of 869. Each of these was sometimes referred to as the "Eighth Synod." But nothing much was made of either until two centuries later when the canons passed in 869 against secular interference in church appointment were found valuable precedents in the conflict then developing between popes and emperors in the West.

ᴥᔄ IV

The ancient ecumenical councils were mainly Eastern in their membership, theological in their interests, and summoned by imperial initiative. The mediaeval Western assemblies which have come to be listed with them were primarily interested in disciplinary questions and were summoned by the popes. The older councils were connected with the heart of the Byzantine Empire around Constantinople. The later ones met at various places in Western Europe, though they can be considered Roman if by "Rome" we mean not only the city on the Tiber but the residence of the Roman Bishop wherever he may be.

The ancient canons called for frequent meetings of provincial councils, Nicaea for instance desired one in the fall and another before Lent so that cases of excommunication might be settled before Easter. The system was never in full operation, but decisions of provincial or national councils are important in the early Middle Ages. The height of organization was perhaps reached in Roman Africa with its numerous bishoprics. Provincial councils met frequently, that of proconsular Africa presided over by the Bishop of Carthage, the others by the senior bishop. From time to time plenary councils or general conventions of all the provinces met, composed (if as usual they met at Carthage) of the bishops of proconsular Africa and delegates from the other provinces. In Gaul there were numerous councils, assembled from rather casually defined, rather than strictly provincial, areas. One that came to be of special importance is the Second Council of Orange (529), whose statements on the doctrine of grace and free-will are often considered as having expressed the general mind of the Church. After the conversion of the Visigoths, the Councils of Toledo were national assemblies in seventh-century Spain, sometimes functioning more as a royal council with clerical members, sometimes as a church assembly with lay representation. Laymen were also present in some capacity at the councils of the Anglo-Saxon Church, which begin with the Council of Hertford assembled by Theodore of Tarsus in 673. Charlemagne carried through many of his ecclesiastical reforms in his capacity as a Christian prince, so that his laws, like Justinian's, cover a wide range of religious as well as secular affairs. But more strictly ecclesiastical assemblies were also important in guiding the discipline of the Church in ninth-century France.

Even in the Tenth Century, when both secular and religious affairs had fallen into great disorder, the conciliar method of legislation was not forgotten. It was ready for use when the eleventh-century popes began to promote a stricter discipline in church affairs. The interventions of the Holy Roman Emperors (now German) were spasmodic even when helpful, and came to be increasingly resented. The policy which we associate with the influence of the Abbey of Cluny called for internal reform of the Church and for independence of the hierarchy from the secular authority. The councils which met at Rome at the beginning of Lent came to be attended by bishops from foreign parts as well as from the local area, and so could be described as "general" in the sense of international. The *Dictatus Papae*, a document which expresses the Roman claims of the time of Gregory VII (1073-1085), lays down the principle that only the pope can authorize a general council (*i.e.*, inter-provincial), and that his approval is needed for the decisions of even provincial assemblies.

Increasingly impressive gatherings of bishops and the almost equally important abbots, sometimes with delegates of cathedral chapters and representatives of princes present as well, were used as instruments of papal policy. Such for instance were the assemblies at Piacenza and Clermont which inaugurated the First Crusade in 1095. For four centuries the launching of crusades was to be, at least in theory, a prime reason for the assembly of councils as a kind of parliament of Western Christendom. The increasing study of canon law may have helped to develop the idea that those gatherings could be considered as continuations of the series of ancient ecumenical synods. The first definitely summoned as such was the First Lateran Council of 1123. The Church of St. John Lateran is the proper cathedral of the Bishop of Rome as such (St. Peter's is a shrine church outside the ancient walls, like Westminster Abbey outside the City of London), and the neighboring palace was his ancient residence. Other Lateran Councils, dealing with questions of church discipline and current affairs, were held in 1139 and 1179. The climax of this series and the formal high-water mark of the mediaeval papal monarchy was reached in the Fourth Lateran Council held under Innocent III in 1215. The Pope seemed at the moment supreme in ecclesiastical affairs and almost equally powerful in political. Four hundred bishops and twice as many abbots responded to his summons to the Council, at whose opening he preached from the text "With desire have I desired to eat this passover with you" (*Luke 22:15*). One unfortunate bishop was killed in the crush at the opening ceremony.

The decisions of the Council were issued in seventy canons, formally passed in three sessions between November 11 and 30. This does not exclude informal discussions between the public sessions, although the Pope probably presented the Council with a draft already prepared. Canon 1, doctrinal in content, is often called the Lateran Creed. It presents the outline which Western theology has since commonly followed—Trinity, Incarnation, Church and Sacraments—and incidentally speaks of the bread and wine of the Eucharist as "transubstantiated" into the Body and Blood of Christ. Against the dualist asceticism of the Albigenses it declares that salvation is open to all, married as well as celibate. It is the mediaeval equivalent of such a document as the Chalcedonian Decree. Its structure may be compared to the magnificence of a Gothic cathedral, or to a work of art like Van Eyck's "Adoration of the Lamb" which also presents the Church of God as a Kingdom in which Christ reigns, both priest and victim. The later canons order many aspects of the life of the Church and her members. Among the more important are those which require annual confession, if necessary, and at least annual communion (21); direct the reverent and safe reservation of the Blessed Sacrament and the holy oils, order the federation of Augustinian and Benedictine monasteries on the lines of the newer orders like the Cistercians (12); direct the bishops to provide for preachers in their dioceses and cathedrals, to support teachers of theology and endeavor to reduce to a reasonable limit the degrees within which marriage was forbidden. Over it all there watches an orderly and systematic, rather conservative mind. Innocent was more concerned, as perhaps a legislator must be, to preserve the achievements of the past than to break new ground. No new monastic orders were to be founded, a provision which made it necessary for St. Dominic to bring his Preaching Friars under the Rule of St. Augustine. Fortunately St. Francis had already secured approval for his more revolutionary foundation some years before.

The apparent success of 1215 was soon followed by a generation of conflict between the Emperor Frederick II and successive popes, which went far to destroy the Empire and discredit the papacy. The popes were often not safe at Rome itself. For over a century they often took refuge in the cities of the Rhone, French in culture and language although at this time not technically part of the Kingdom of France. Here in 1245 Innocent IV assembled a Council at Lyons, the main business of which was to declare the deposition of Frederick. When the struggle with Frederick's heirs finally ended in 1268, the great institutions of mediaeval Europe were exhausted. The Empire, vacant since 1250, was not filled till the election of Rudolf of Habsburg in 1273, and there was a three-years interregnum before the papal chair was filled by the choice of Gregory X in 1271. Though an Italian, he was Archdeacon of Liege. But at the moment of his election he was in Acre, the center of the remaining fragment of the crusading kingdom in Palestine; among his associates there was Prince Edward who was shortly to return to succeed his father on the English throne as Edward I, the last English crusading prince and the first great English national monarch. Gregory summoned a council to Lyons, where it assembled in 1274. Its most conspicuous business was a request for reunion from the Greeks, who in 1261 had recovered and ended the Latin Empire which had been set up in 1204 by the misguided adventure of the Fourth Crusade. The two great theologians of the age were both summoned to advise the Council, though both died in this year—Thomas Aquinas on his way to the Council, Bonaventura after being consecrated to the episcopate as Cardinal Bishop of Albano, while joining in its proceedings. The Fourth Crusade had completed the schism which began with the breach of Communion between Pope and Patriarch in 1054. The formal effort at reunion constituted an admission that the situation had hardened. The Greek Emperor Michael seems to have had little real interest in achieving unity or even in discussing the *filioque*, but was mainly concerned to make diplomatic gestures which would prevent papal support being given to Latin claimants to the imperial throne. In this he was successful. But though the union was formally inaugurated, and had some sincere supporters, including the Patriarch of Constantinople, it is best described as a premature and abortive effort, soon forgotten after Michael's death in 1281. Other measures of the Council were rules for speeding up papal elections, and a recognition of the four great orders of Friars (Franciscans, Dominicans, Carmelites, and Augustinians), suppressing all others. Whether Gregory X might have obtained something like the success of Innocent III if he had lived longer is possible but doubtful; times were changing. In any case, after his death in 1276 no successor of comparable ability appeared.

The mediaeval effort at political and intellectual synthesis was visibly beginning to fail when Acre fell in 1291.

Already the national monarchy was succeeding the international Empire and the Crusade as the center of political enterprise. Boniface VIII (1294-1303) attempted in vain in the Bull *Unam Sanctam* (1302) to assert his supremacy over Christendom in civil as well as ecclesiastical affairs. He was defied and insulted by the agents of Philip the Fair of France, and his successors for two generations were dominated by the French kings. Councils which were instruments of papal policy were followed by councils which were means of controlling the pope. To regularize the new state of affairs Clement V called a council which met at Vienne, south of Lyons, in 1311-12. Its decisions were to some extent a compromise. Clement avoided a formal condemnation of his predecessor Boniface VIII, but was obliged to accept the suppression of the international military Order of the Templars, who had lost their reason for being with the loss of Palestine. Other actions were little more than pious gestures, such as the measure urged by the mystic and missionary Ramon Lull calling on the universities to establish chairs of oriental languages for the benefit of missions. This deserves mention, however, as symbolic of the spiritual crusade of later centuries which would mean more for the Church than the military crusades of the past. But at the moment the missionary zeal which had taken friars as far as Cambaluc, known to us as Peiping, was dying down, and the advance of the Turks increasingly cut off communications between Europe and the Orient.

As the Ignatian and Photian Councils of the Ninth Century are a kind of appendage to the ancient councils and a foretaste of mediaeval developments, so the Council of Vienne is a kind of appendage to the papal councils of the

Middle Ages and a foretaste of the reforming councils of the Fifteenth Century. The immediate results were slight however. The popes continued in their French exile, and after some years took up the residence in Avignon from which this period has acquired the name of the Avignon captivity. The rivalry of John XXII (1316-1334) and the Emperor Louis of Bavaria is a kind of muffled echo of the more heroic struggles of previous centuries. From the groups connected with Louis, however, came literary supporters of the theory that ultimate authority in the visible Church does not belong to the pope or even to the hierarchy as such, but to a general council of all Christians. Circumstances were soon to produce an occasion for acting on this theory.

◅§ V

Though no longer as impressive as it had been, the papacy was still the organ of ecclesiastical unity in Western Europe and the symbol at least of international amity. Hence it was a political as well as a religious problem when the papacy itself was split by the disputed election of 1378. Gregory XI had at last returned to Rome from the Avignonese exile the year before, and on his death the cardinals responded to the appeal of the people, "Give us a Roman, or at least an Italian." On discovering the harshness of the Archbishop of Bari, who had become Urban VI, the electors slipped away one by one. Then on the ground that they had acted under duress they held another election and chose Robert of Geneva, who took the name of Clement VII. There was much to be said for each side. But the practical result was to split the Church along mainly national lines between Urban and his successors at Rome and Clement at Avignon. Each party could consider the other schismatic; but since no matter of principle was involved it became customary to use a milder term and speak of the Church as divided into rival "obediences." This is the first anticipation, I believe, of our modern recognition that to some extent at least the Church is in a state of mutual schism, between parties divided from each other, of which neither is clearly and entirely right or wrong.

But in the Fourteenth Century division was still not accepted, and all agreed that the "Great Schism of the West" needed to be resolved. It soon became clear that this would not be by a victory of one side or the other (*per viam facti*), and by 1400 efforts to secure a solution by the abdication of one or both claimants (*per viam cessionis*) had also failed. There remained the possibility of calling on the whole body to bring its unruly heads to order, acting in a general council, *per viam concilii*. Promoted theoretically and practically by theologians of the University of Paris, this was taken up by cardinals of both parties who summoned a Council which met at Pisa in 1409. It is worth noting that three important corporate bodies felt driven at this time to the deposition of their heads. In England, Richard II was deposed for misgovernment by Parliament in 1399—in the Holy Roman Empire the electors revoked in the same year their choice of the Emperor Wenzel (for drunkenness)— and the Church endeavored to set its house in order by a similar revolutionary step ten years later. As in the English and American Revolutions of 1688 and 1776, the unprece-

dented character of the step was mitigated by an appeal to
ancient principles of law. It was argued that by neglecting to
heal the Schism, the rival popes had shown that they did
not really believe in one Church, and so forfeited their
rights by heresy. But by all the principles of church government then understood the project was a revolutionary one.

The Council of Pisa selected as pope an aged Franciscan
from Crete (then under Venetian rule) as Alexander V. He
was shortly succeeded by a less respectable figure, Baldassare
Cossa, who had been an efficient military commander in the
papal states but was scarcely fitted for the priesthood, still
less for the position which he assumed in 1410 as John
XXIII. There were now three parties, since the Roman
claimant retained some support and the Avignonese a good
deal. But the Council of Pisa had been a step forward, and
the remedy now sought was a more generally supported
council, to meet in German territory, which was neutral or
at least divided. John, backed by the Emperor Sigismund,
was persuaded to summon a council to meet at Constance
on All Saints' Day 1414. When it began business, some
months later, it was the most representative gathering of
the mediaeval Church, and, one might say, the first of the
international conferences of modern times which have
found Swiss or adjoining territory a convenient central meeting point. To avoid predominance of the numerous Italian
bishops, the Council adopted the method of voting by "nations" or geographical areas, with which most of the members had been familiar in the student body proceedings of
mediaeval universities. There were at first four nations, Italian, German, French, and English, other countries being
attached to one or another; later five when the Spanish

bishops abandoned the Avignon obedience and appeared at the Council.

The Council of Constance remained in session for nearly three years, for most of which it was in fact the highest authority in the Church. It claimed that it was such anyway by the decree *Sacrosancta* affirming that the General Council "duly convened in the Holy Spirit" held supreme power in the Church for the definition of the faith and also for the reformation of the Church in head and members. All three claimants were eliminated. John XXIII was deposed on moral grounds, escaped from Constance, and then returned to accept his deposition. The Roman claimant, Gregory XII, was persuaded by his chief supporter, the Prince of Rimini, to re-summon the Council by his authority, and then to abdicate to it. The second Avignon claimant, Benedict XIII, was an aged canonist, Pedro de Luna, the last survivor of the cardinals of 1378. He was formally declared deposed, France abandoned him and, having lived through the whole period of schism, he took refuge in his native Aragon (still maintaining his claim till his death in 1424). It seems clear in retrospect that the Roman succession had the better canonical claim, even though in 1410-15 it had little support; the Avignon popes were ignored in the numbering of later popes who took the names Clement and Benedict—and, while to avoid confusion the next Pope Alexander called himself Alexander VI, on his election in 1958 Cardinal Roncalli ignored the 15th-century John and took the name John XXIII.

The Council was less successful in undertaking positive re-form of the Church (the word should always be used in reference to this period with a sense of its etymology, the shaping of a new form of spiritual life and church discipline). It tried to restrict in favor of bishops the expensive administrative operations of the papal court, but had nothing more efficient, still less anything more spiritual, to put in their place. The radical criticism of the external Church which had been begun by Wycliffe in England and taken up by Hus in Bohemia came before it. But its only action was to demonstrate its orthodoxy by burning the heretic who, under better guidance, might have been used as a loyal reformer. Its only program for the future was that councils like itself should meet frequently, one in five years, another after seven, and then others at ten-year intervals, a rule laid down in the appropriately-named decree *Frequens*. Rather wearily the Council turned to the election of a new pope, for which on this occasion six doctors of Divinity from each nation joined the twenty-six cardinals present. Cardinal Odo Colonna was elected on St. Martin's Day, November 11, 1417, and in recognition of the date took the name of Martin V. It is an interesting coincidence that the mediaeval Church had almost exactly a century left to re-form itself before Martin Luther, so christened because he had been born near the festival, posted his Ninety-Five Theses on the Eve of All Saints' in 1517.

To those who hope that the Spirit will speak through an ordered constitutional government in the family of the Church, the story of the fifteenth-century conciliar movement is a warning and a disappointment. As an emergency measure, the councils reconstituted the papacy; they did not succeed in re-forming the Church. In part this is because their methods and aims were political rather than spiritual. In part their good intentions were over-ridden by the spirit of the Renaissance with its admiration of the decisive individual, producing an age in which autocracy seemed to be the alternative to anarchy.

Martin V was equally active in restoring his control in the papal states and his power in the Church. However, in accordance with the decree *Frequens* he did summon a council to meet at Siena. But it was poorly attended and shortly dissolved. Before his death in 1430 he had summoned a council to meet at Basle, which hesitantly convened in the following year. Once more the place of meeting was beside the Rhine on the northern side of the Swiss mountains. Beginning hesitantly, the Council was dissolved by Martin's successor Eugenius IV. However, it refused to accept his decision and was again allowed to proceed. In due time a fair number of bishops and abbots were assembled—and a number of other members who were supposed to be doctors of divinity "incorporated" into the Council. But it was suspected that miscellaneous hangers-on were allowed to put on gowns and join the assembly when an impressive session was desired. Basle was not so much a council as a battleground between the Pope and his rivals. It attempted to seize control of the papal administration but achieved only a few harmless pieces of legislation, such as rules for the behavior of cathedral clergy in choir; for instance their surplices should be ample, reaching at least to the shin.

The Council finally broke in two over the issue of negotiation with the Greeks. Constantinople had gone on its own way ecclesiastically since 1282. In the Fourteenth Century it had held councils of its own on the controversy raised by the theology of Gregory Palamas of Thessalonica, one of which is sometimes referred to (honorifically) as an "Eighth

General Council." Speaking very roughly, the Greeks decided in favor of their traditional mystical-Platonic approach to Theology as opposed to the rationalistic-Aristotelian of Thomas Aquinas—the episode illustrates poignantly the loss to both parts of the Church in their isolation from each other. But now the Byzantine Empire, reduced to the City of Constantine and a few parts of Greece, was in its last extremity. The need for help against the Turks joined with the genuine interest of a few in reunion with the Latin Church to lead to approaches on the subject. It was still assumed that as in the days of the Crusades Western Christendom would act as a unit under its ecclesiastical leaders. But the rather amusing question now was, who were they? Embassies from Basle and Eugenius both went to Constantinople. The Greeks had little difficulty in deciding in favor of the single authority, and in 1437 a large delegation headed by Emperor and Patriarch set out for Italy. To meet them at a convenient point Eugenius formally transferred the Council to Ferrara.

There are hereafter two councils, each of which must briefly be followed to its end. Early in 1439 the papal Council was transferred to Florence, which was better prepared to accommodate it. Here amid Renaissance splendors the union was formally proclaimed on July 6, 1439. The principle of the "Florentine Union" is that still propounded by the papacy for reunion with the Eastern Churches—acceptance of Roman doctrine and ultimate authority, with recognition of Eastern rites and rights, *i.e.*, liturgical customs and the position of the Patriarchs. The Union was barely accepted at Constantinople, and lapsed after the fall of the city in 1453. There might conceivably have been a different development if the crusading expedition (mainly Hungarian) which marched into Bulgaria had met with victory instead of disaster at the Battle of Varna in 1444. After the Greeks left, a similar decree was issued for the Armenians, whose delegates seem actually to have come only from Caffa in the Crimea, then a Genoese colony. The document is best known because it contains the instruction on the Sacraments which, among other things, states that the *traditio instrumentorum* (delivery of chalice and patent) is the essential form of ordination to the priesthood (a view changed in our time by Pius XII, who returned in 1948 to the older view that laying-on of hands and appropriate prayer are the essentials). Even more obscure delegates appeared from the Coptic and Ethiopian Churches. In 1443 the Pope took the Council back with him to Rome, from which he had been exiled since 1434. Formal sessions were held there for representatives of the Syrian Jacobites, and the Chaldeans and Maronites of Cyprus. Without being formally adjourned, the papal Council of Basle-Ferrara-Florence-Rome ceased to act after 1445. Eugenius could claim when he died in 1447 that he had reunited the Church. The papacy embarked on its Renaissance glories, so soon to be tarnished by the secular and political interests of the next generation.

The rump session, as we may call it, at Basle, abandoned none of its claims, although the national sovereigns increasingly preferred to do business with the Pope rather than supporting an opposition to him. In 1439 the Council professed to depose Eugenius. Only one cardinal being present (Louis Aleman, Archbishop of Arles), it set up an electoral college which on November 5 chose to the office a curious ecclesiastically-minded layman, Amadeus VIII, late Duke of Savoy. As Felix V he became the last anti-pope of history, the end of a series which goes back to the earliest disputed elections to the Roman see in the Third Century. With decreasing support he functioned for some years at Basle, and then at Lausanne. Here the Council was allowed to expire with some dignity in 1449, accepting Felix's abdication and going through the form of electing Tommaso da Sarzana, who had already succeeded Eugenius IV at Rome as Nicholas V. In 1460 the next Pope, Pius II, who had been first the servant and then the opponent of the Council of Basle, condemned the anti-papal phase of the conciliar movement by the prohibition in his bull *Execrabilis* of appeals from the pope to a future general council. He did not formally reverse the position of the decree *Sacrosancta*, on the power of a council in session, but declared that appeals to a future council were improper, in view of the final authority given to Peter and his successors to bind and loose; and useless, since they were addressed to a body which did not exist at the moment and whose future meeting was uncertain.

◄§ VI

By 1500 it could not be denied that the Western Church needed a more serious re-form than the fifteenth-century councils had achieved or even aimed at. The scandals of the Roman court in the 1490's are only one indication that a rethinking of doctrine as well as a renewal of discipline was called for. In the Sixteenth Century this came in diverse ways to the different parts of the Western Church, but unhappily at the expense of further divisions. Protestantism in its two main forms of the Evangelical (Lutheran) and Reformed (Calvinist) Churches, and others more radical, the English Reformation, and the Counter-Reformation within the Roman Communion—all these can in some ways be considered as aspects of the same movement, or at least as responses to the same need. At certain stages all parties looked to a general council as the desired instrument of reform. Curiously enough one was, technically, actually in session at the time which we think of as the eve of the Reformation. Political plums connected with the French invasions of Italy were mainly behind Louis XII's appeal to a general council in 1510, in response to which a small assembly convened at Pisa in 1511. By way of counterblast Julius II summoned a council to Rome which, as the Fifth Lateran, met at intervals from 1512-1517. There are some interesting items in its proceedings, such as the declaration of the immortality of the soul (against neo-pagan scepticism), but otherwise its results were limited to a few minor regulations.

Nevertheless the recent session of a council may explain why the demand for one came naturally to such diverse proponents of reform as Martin Luther and Henry VIII. Sometimes the call for a council is more a means of repudiating ultimate papal authority than a serious positive proposal. Luther's phrase, for instance, about a "free Christian Council on German soil," though it seems to pick up the fifteenth-century precedents, was not to be taken as a very serious suggestion. It would have presumably been something like Basle, a meeting free from papal control and with lay participation (as had sometimes been proposed in the Fifteenth Century) or at least under lay influence. In the disputes which followed his posting of the *Theses* Luther found himself defending some of John Hus's positions and therefore obliged to maintain that the Council of Constance had erred in condemning him. Henceforth he and his followers could accept no final authority except the Word of God as they found it in the Bible. However this did not exclude common statements of convictions, of which the first was the Augsburg Confession of 1530. This is technically a lay document, in that though drawn up by theologians, it was submitted to the Imperial Diet by the Lutheran princes and towns in justification of their protest against the edict putting Luther under the ban of the Empire.

Under Paul III (1534-1549) the forces of reform began to come to the front within the Roman Communion as well as among those who were breaking away from it. The Pope promised to call a general council for the reform of the Church, and for a while there was some hope that this might be a conciliatory gathering. But the effort of well-disposed theologians on either side to come to an understanding at the Colloquy of Ratisbon (1541) merely indicated that the breach between Catholics and Lutherans had become definite. The Council which finally met at Trent was committed to consolidating and defining the Roman Catholic position. Some wished to give the first place to doctrine, others to discipline. In 1545-7 decrees on Scripture and Tradition, on Justification, and on the Sacraments clarified and enforced the positions inherited from the Middle Ages; and by agreement the dogmatic decrees were each accompanied by canons on measures of practical reform.

The history of the Council of Trent is complex and at times stormy. The site represented a certain compromise—

it was technically a German territory but on the Italian side of the Alps. On the ground of an outbreak of plague the sessions were transferred to Bologna in 1548, but no decrees were issued there. Under the next Pope, Julius III, sessions were resumed at Trent in 1551-52, interrupted this time by the threatening advance of Protestant armies. From 1555-1559 the Pope was Paul IV, a reformer who had become so conservative that he regarded even an orthodox council with suspicion. His successor, Pius IV, desired to complete the work of the Council, but was delayed by the hesitation of the French, previously unrepresented, as to whether they would take part in it or not. In 1561, a conference organized by the French court at Poissy, near Paris, attempted in vain to find a basis of agreement between Catholics and Calvinists. When this failed the religious divisions in France became definite, as those in Germany had twenty years before, and French bishops were allowed to take part in the resumed sessions at Trent. Rather like our modern legislatures, the Council took care of a great deal of business in its final sessions, 1562-3; these dealt largely with the organization of dioceses and the administration of the Sacraments. Two days were required for the reading of the miscellaneous decrees formally passed in the final session, December 3-4, 1563.

Although poorly attended in its first two periods, the Council of Trent represented the best thought of those who remained in the Roman Communion. Only superiors of religious orders were voting members in addition to the bishops, but others present as theological advisers were at times even more influential. Papal legates presided but, in spite of a joke about the guidance of the Holy Spirit arriving by mail from Rome, this did not prevent vigorous discussions and even stormy debates. Out of the Tridentine meetings did emerge the solid pattern of Counter-Reformation Catholicism—a Church like the building of St. Peter's at Rome, "militant, expectant, and all but triumphant," as a modern historian has put it.* Those who differ on important points, or still find that the Tridentine synthesis is not the whole truth, must still credit it with a certain magnificence.

The Seventeenth and Eighteenth centuries saw a series of non-Roman dogmatic statements issued with the authority of national or regional assemblies. Such were the Thirty-Nine Articles of the Church of England, adopted by the Convocation of Canterbury in 1563, and the series of Calvinist Confessions from the French *Confessio Gallicana* of 1559 to the Westminster Confession and associated documents. These last were drafted in 1642-6 by the Assembly of Divines which met with a view to the proposed Presbyterian reorganization of the Church of England, but in the event adopted by the Church of Scotland and others related to it. Two gatherings which have somewhat the character of general councils are worth mentioning. The Synod of Dort, convened by the Reformed Church of Holland in 1618-9, was called to pass judgment on the weakening of strict Calvinism in the theology of Arminius. Besides the Dutch, it had German and Swiss delegates and even English and Scottish, though these represented their theologically-minded monarch, James I and VI, rather than their Churches as such. The Canons of Dort enunciate the strict-

* Leighton Pullan, *Religion Since the Reformation* (London: Oxford, 1923), p. 12.

est doctrines of absolute predestination, and as the "five points of Calvinism" have been vigorously held and vigorously opposed. At the other end of the Christian world the Greek Church suffered from both protestantizing and romanizing influences, against both of which a council of the four ancient Patriarchates assembled at Jerusalem in 1672 (also sometimes called the Synod of Bethlehem, from where it was originally summoned). Under the leadership of the Patriarch Dositheos of Jerusalem, this adopted a statement of the Orthodox faith in the current form of a series of articles. Though traditional in content, this *Confessio Dosithei* is influenced in form and terminology (as could also be said of the XXXIX Articles) by the pattern of the times—as for instance by introducing the term "transubstantiation" into Orthodox usage, in which it has never been quite at home.

With these proceedings the conciliar technique may be said to die down for nearly two centuries. The idea however was kept alive by the Gallican movement within the Latin Church, one of whose principles (as formulated by Bossuet in 1682) was that the ultimate authority in matters of doctrine does not lie with pope but with general council. The principle was given some practical application a generation later by French bishops and others who were sympathetic with the Jansenist party (best described briefly as Catholic Puritans), or at least critical of the condemnation of a Jansenist devotional work in the Bull *Unigenitus,* issued in 1713. Against the condemnation a number of bishops and superiors formally appealed to the next general council, and therefore are described as Appellants. Suspected of Jansenism, the Church of Utrecht was unable to secure consecration for its Archbishop-elect. A French missionary bishop agreed to perform the ceremony in 1724, and thus began the separate existence of what has become the Old Catholic Communion.

This story however belongs to the Nineteenth Century, and to the Catholic revival which followed the blows of the French Revolution and the Napoleonic era. The movement generally is a broad one, a revival of traditional churchmanship after the rationalism or pietism of the Eighteenth Century. It appeared in different forms in the Church of England, in various parts of Protestantism, and in the Eastern Orthodox Churches. In the Roman Communion there are two aspects of the movement, one tending more to reach out into the modern world, the other to call for renewed loyalty to the papal authority. To these the names Liberal Catholic and Ultramontane (*i.e.*, from the viewpoint of northern Europe, supporters of the pope "over the mountains") are often given, though somewhat confusedly. Pius IX (1846-78) began his pontificate with a relatively liberal policy. But after his expulsion from Rome by the revolutionary forces of 1848 he threw his weight on the side of political conservatism and ecclesiastical centralization. He had the advantage of being the first pope for whom the facilities of communication by steam and telegraph were completely available; the disadvantage of associating his religious policy in the minds of many with what was, as it turned out, the doomed political effort to maintain his civil sovereignty in the Papal States. In 1854 he acted on the view, widely held but never before explicitly put into practice, that the pope could by himself define dogma in the name of the Church. The Immaculate Conception of the

Blessed Virgin was promulgated as an article of the faith after consultation with the episcopate, but in the Pope's own authority. Numerous papal pronouncements of a less solemn character, which in general seemed to be a defiance of the "liberal" tendencies of the day, were summarized in the *Syllabus of Errors* issued in 1864.

However Pius IX still wished to act with the greater solemnity of a council. After several preliminary announcements, in 1868 he summoned the Vatican Council which convened at St. Peter's on December 8, 1869 (Feast of the Immaculate Conception). The original plan was to consider a great variety of dogmatic and disciplinary matters, which might have occupied the 774 bishops present for several years. Many of the canonical and liturgical reforms proposed have since been carried into effect. But it took the Council four months to produce its first dogmatic decree, on Reason and Revelation and belief in God, proclaimed on April 24, 1870. A *schema* on the Church was next brought forward. But since the sessions continued to drag on, the subject of most concern to Pius IX and his closest supporters, the primacy and infallibility of the pope, was brought forward out of turn. Those present had no objection to the former doctrine in the form that the Bishop of Rome has true direct episcopal authority over every believer; it is perhaps more of a barrier between Roman and non-Roman Christendom than the very cautiously worded statement on infallibility which finally appeared. The latter was opposed by a large minority, including many bishops of important dioceses. Most of the minority, however, professed only to doubt the wisdom of defining the proposition as a dogma, not its actual truth. In a General Congregation, corresponding to Committee of the Whole, on July 11 there were 451 votes for the definition, 88 against, and 62 for it with modifications. Most of the leaders of the minority left before the formal session on July 18 when the decree was adopted by 535 votes to two (the Bishops of Little Rock in Arkansas and Cajazzo in Dalmatia)—I suspect this was a prearranged symbolic protest.

On the following day the Franco-Prussian War broke out and the bishops dispersed. The French troops who had protected the papacy since 1860 were withdrawn. Two months later the Italian troops occupied Rome and the Pope took up the position of "prisoner of the Vatican" which he and his successors maintained until 1929. Most of the minority bishops accepted the Vatican decree immediately, although several who had been genuinely opposed to the doctrine of papal infallibility hesitated for some time. The Old Catholics of the German-speaking countries were, however, able to secure the episcopate from Holland and thus organize the German, Swiss, and Austrian Churches of the Old Catholic Communion. The Council was never formally declared dissolved, but may be presumed to have ended with the ultimate death of all its members. General councils then passed out of current concern until on January 25, 1959, Pope John XXIII announced his intention of summoning another.

Perhaps it was just as well that the Vatican Council adjourned with its major task unaccomplished, since no part of Christendom was well prepared at that time for a formulation of the Church's doctrine about herself. We can perhaps see in our own century the prospects of an ultimate convergence of the traditions which have so long been competing rivals—in the growth within the "great Latin Church of the West" (so described by the Lambeth Conference of 1920) of a fuller understanding of the corporate and social character of Christian worship and life, which shows the nineteenth-century Liberal Catholics and Ultramontanes as both tainted with individualism—in the increasing understanding between Christians produced through the Ecumenical Movement, especially by its Conferences on Faith and Order (which with symbolic appropriateness began in 1927 at Lausanne, where the fifteenth-century conciliar movement had expired in 1449)—and in the return of the Eastern Churches to friendly dialogue with those of Western tradition. Perhaps the world may yet see the realization, if not in our time, of the hopes expressed by a Scottish bishop on the eve of the assembly of the Council of the Vatican:

> as in the century preceding the Reformation, earnest men of all hues of opinion looked forward to the assembling of a General Council as the great cure of the evils of the day, so now may not we, laying to heart the great dangers we are in from our unhappy divisions, hope, and labour and pray for the hour when the Church of God shall again come together in its glory and strength, when, compelled by the crushing assaults of the common foe, and animated by the earnest desire of peace, all who believe in the Divinity of our Blessed Saviour, and in the necessity of a visible Church as His organ, shall assemble under the guidance of God Himself . . . (Bishop Forbes of Brechin, quoted in H.T.R. Brandreth, *The Oecumenical Ideals of the Oxford Movement*, S.P.C.K., 1947, p. 54).

✑ VII

It remains in this historical section to add some notes on the composition, procedure, and authority of general councils. Our comments may conveniently start with the statement of the Thirty-Nine Articles that "The Church hath power to decree Rites or Ceremonies, and authority in Controversies of Faith" as "a witness and a keeper of Holy Writ" (Article XX), to which follows, in the English form, Article XXI:

> General Councils may not be gathered together without the commandment and will of Princes. And when they be gathered together, (forasmuch as they be an assembly of men, whereof all be not governed with the Spirit and Word of God,) they may err, and sometimes have erred, even in things pertaining unto God. Wherefore things ordained by them as necessary to salvation have neither strength nor authority, unless it may be declared that they be taken out of Holy Scripture.

In the American version this Article is omitted, as being partly covered in others and partly "of a local and civil nature." It does indeed take us back to England in the early years of Queen Elizabeth I, and was specifically intended to challenge the authority of the Council of Trent, at that time in session.

We would not now speak of the "commandment and will of Princes" quite so easily—although Trent could indeed have claimed that, because its first two groups of sessions were supported by Charles V in his capacity of Holy Roman Emperor. What the phrase really indicates is that a general council in ancient times was an act of the whole

Church and not of any order within it. Constantine and his successors may be considered as the embodiment of the laity, calling upon bishops and theologians to discharge their particular responsibilities. On the whole it was better when the Christian sovereign was not himself a theologian —neither Justinian nor James I were very happy in their incursions into this sphere. But the sovereign expressed the action of the whole body by calling for the council and then endorsing its results. This basically corporate character of the whole affair was really more significant than the actual membership of the council. In principle councils of the Church are meetings of bishops, but other clergy and laymen have been present in one capacity or another. Even the Greek delegation at the Council of Florence reflected a flexibility in such matters which is familiar in the Eastern Churches today. It was headed jointly by the Emperor John VIII and the Patriarch Joseph (until the death of the latter at Florence), and lay theologians as well as clerical took part in the discussions. Even at Trent the ambassadors of Catholic sovereigns played a significant part. The purely clerical character of the mediaeval papal councils and of those envisaged by modern Roman Canon Law is not in accordance with ancient precedent.

The procedure of councils has naturally been in accordance with that of whatever kind of deliberative assembly contemporaries were used to. The Council of Jerusalem acted like a Greek civic assembly, and the ancient general councils followed a procedure based on that of the Roman Senate. There was not precisely our modern distinction between debate and voting, but when a proposition was put forward those present expressed their opinions in order of rank. The crucial problem might be not so much who presided as who spoke first. Thus at Chalcedon the imperial commissioners who sat in front were less important than the first speakers, the Patriarch of Constantinople and the Roman delegates. The mediaeval councils had somewhat the character of a feudal court, in which the lord gave his decision after listening to the views of his vassals. The fifteenth-century councils resembled the assemblies of Estates, in which the main problem was to secure agreement among the different elements represented. Trent is one of the first cases of modern parliamentary procedure, with special committees, general discussions, and finally formal voting. The Vatican Council also acted under parliamentary rules. This allowed for some manipulation (as when Archbishop Manning of Westminster secured the election of twenty-three Ultramontanes to the select committee of twenty-four on matters of faith), but also allowed for long debates which at times almost reached the stage of a filibuster. Future councils may have to look for guidance to assemblies like those of the United Nations, especially since they will, unfortunately perhaps, not be able to count on Greek or Latin as common tongues for discussion and debate.

A question of importance to theologians and historians, and also from a practical point of view, is how one can tell that a particular gathering has in fact been a general council and truly spoken the mind of the Church. This involves the further point whether it is ever possible for the members of a council to be sure in advance that they are subscribing to a document to which the Church will be permanently committed. Since the Middle Ages Roman Canon

Law has seemed to give an unequivocal answer: when the pope has summoned a council and then confirmed its decrees, the matter is settled; and any doctrines it has defined are forever binding. So one of the English bishops at the Vatican council noted that, in spite of its vigorous discussions,

> As a rule, the listening assembly has been very silently conscious that it was giving the last touch to decrees of Faith that could never again be changed, and that were to stand, and to which the Church must stand, all days, even to the end of the world. (Bishop Ullathorne of Birmingham, quoted in Cuthbert Butler, *The Vatican Council*, 2 vols., 1930, vol. I, p. 292)

But even here there are degrees of certainty, not to mention the possibility of further reinterpretation or supplementing of what has been said. Eugenius IV's *Instructio ad Armenos* was issued with full conciliar solemnity. Yet its famous pronouncement on the essential ceremony of ordination to the priesthood continued to be discussed, and was quietly superseded by Pius XII in 1948. It seems clear to declare that when the pope speaks *ex cathedra* as teacher of the universal Church on matters of faith and morals, it is claimed that he speaks "with that infallibility with which the Redeemer willed that his Church should be endowed." But even this statement is qualified, not only by the last clause but by the admitted uncertainty as to the frequency of occasions on which he has so spoken.

It seems to be truer to the facts of history to consider that even the most confident decision of a general council is really a question rather than an answer. Its status depends on whether it secures the desired acceptance, or perhaps one should better say recognition, by the Church at large. One may thus put into the picture the rival councils which preceded or followed almost every one of the ancient ecumenical synods. The Church answered "Yes" to Nicaea and "No" to its Arian counterparts, and so with others down to the iconoclastic synods which were repudiated in 787 and 843. From the Eastern point of view Florence, though its acts were published as those of the Eighth Ecumenical Council, was only a question to which the Orthodox mind answered with a resounding negative. What constitutes general recognition by the Church is itself a question not capable of precise answer, though it may be noted that all of the ancient synods received sooner or later the approval of the five patriarchal sees of Rome, Constantinople, Alexandria, Antioch, and Jerusalem. Rome, whose prominence in conciliar history cannot have escaped the reader of these pages, may be considered to have lost its leadership in the whole Church by grasping for autocratic control in a part of it, even if it be a large and impressive section. The Eastern Orthodox Church holds, I believe, in theory that it is indeed the true Church and so would be capable of acting in an ecumenical council. But in practice it has not since 787 claimed such status for a council which has not received Roman approval, nor accepted it for the Roman synods which have been called General, from the Twelfth Century to the Nineteenth. Some Anglican writers use the term "ecumenical council" for the seven (or six) which have received undoubted approval, and "general council" for those which profess to represent the whole Church; but, as Article XXI reminds us, are capable of erring. The soundest general principle, even though it does not offer us the prospect of easy answers to our questions, is probably that enunciated by the Greek Patriarchs in reply to an appeal from Pius IX, that the whole body of the Christian people are the guardians and defenders of the true faith. Historian and theologian may perhaps agree that God has led his Church in many ways—sometimes by conciliar decisions accepted after very human disputes (for God can make even the wrath of man to praise him), sometimes by the slow spread of a common conviction which saints and scholars formulate but the holy people of God ultimately give authority to. The Church is neither a political democracy nor an earthly autocracy. It is something more wonderful than either, the Family of God and the Kingdom of his Son, the Fellowship of the Holy Ghost.